Journey Through Scotland

by Ross Finlay

HAMLYN
London · New York · Sydney · Toronto

Endpapers: The waters of Loch Lomond
Title page: The Pass of Ryvoan
Title verso/Introduction: Mountain scenery at
Glencoe
Contents page: The palace of Linlithgow, West
Lothian

Editor: Donna Wood
Art Editor: Edward Pitcher
Designer: Gordon Robertson
Maps: Eugene Fleury
Production: Steve Roberts

Published 1986 by Hamlyn Publishing, a division of
The Hamlyn Publishing Group Limited, Bridge House,
London Road, Twickenham, Middlesex, England.

©Marshall Cavendish Limited 1986
Produced by Marshall Cavendish Books Limited
ISBN 0-600-50250-3

The contents of this book are believed correct at the time
of printing. Nevertheless, the publisher can accept no
responsibility for errors or omissions or changes in the
details given.

Typeset in Palatino by TypeFast Ltd, London.
Printed in Italy by L.E.G.O. S.p.a. Vicenza.

Introduction

Scotland is a country of extremes and contrasts, incorporating not only some of the wildest and most remote countryside in the British Isles, but some of the most heavily industrialised areas too. Heather-clad, purple Highlands, wild, rugged and relatively unpopulated, and the forlorn, strangely-named islands in the lonely north give way to the bustling, attractive cities of Edinburgh and Glasgow, full of history and bursting with life. High mountains which attract the ski set, and haunting lochs which are said to harbour monsters are all here in this royal country favoured by the British monarchy.

Divided into eight regions, this book describes the well-known tourist honeypots, but throws in some off-the-beaten-track surprises for good measure; the more to make your journey through Scotland a colourful and rewarding one.

Contents

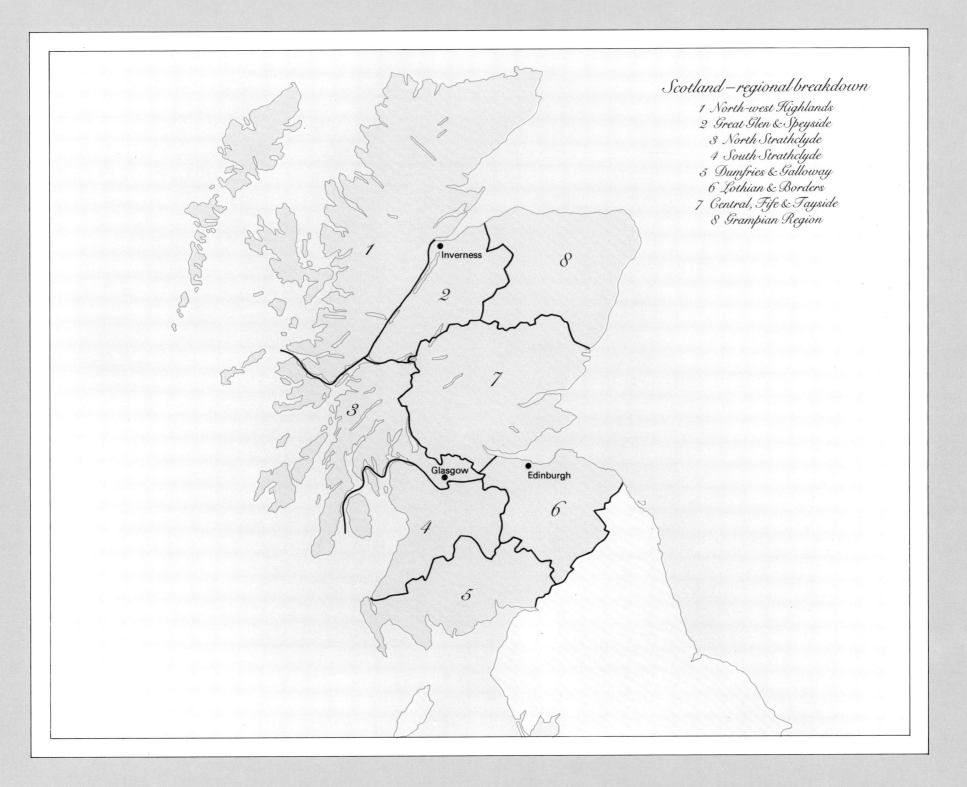

Scotland—regional breakdown
1 North-west Highlands
2 Great Glen & Speyside
3 North Strathclyde
4 South Strathclyde
5 Dumfries & Galloway
6 Lothian & Borders
7 Central, Fife & Tayside
8 Grampian Region

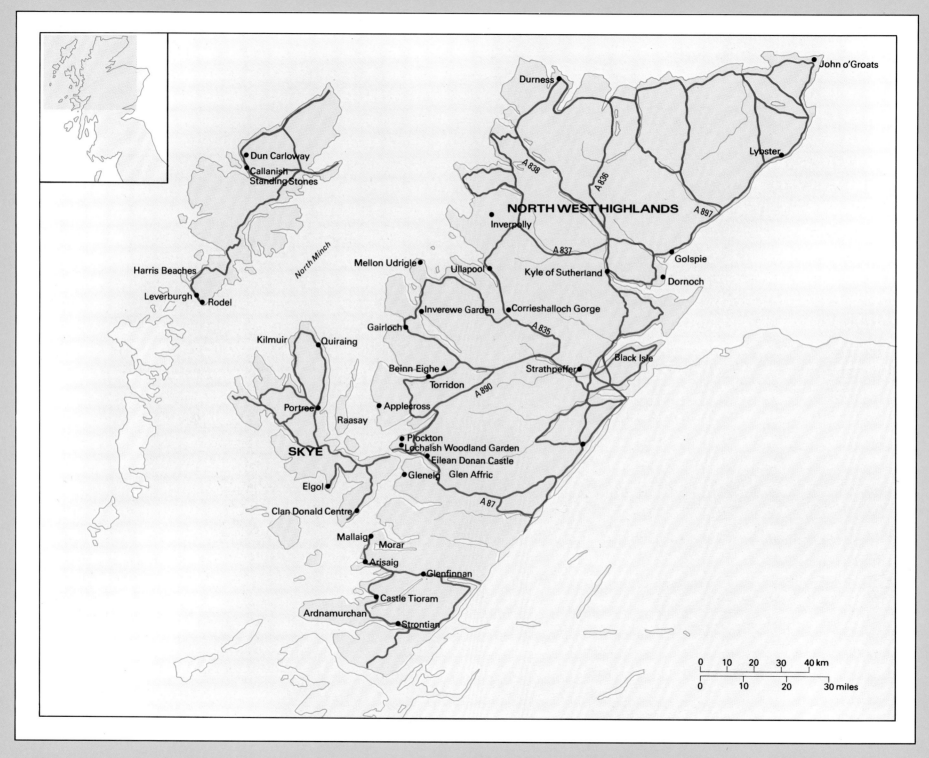

Dun Carloway
Callanish
Standing Stones

North Minch

Harris Beaches
Leverburgh • Rodel

Durness

John o'Groats

A 838

A 836

A 897

Lybster

NORTH WEST HIGHLANDS

Inverpolly

A 837

Golspie

Mellon Udrigle
Ullapool
Kyle of Sutherland
Dornoch

Inverewe Garden
Corrieshalloch Gorge

Gairloch

A 835

Kilmuir Quiraing

Beinn Eighe ▲

Black Isle

Strathpeffer

Torridon

A 890

Portree

Applecross

Raasay

SKYE

Plockton
Lochalsh Woodland Garden
Eilean Donan Castle

Elgol

Glenelg Glen Affric

A 87

Clan Donald Centre

Mallaig

Morar

Arisaig Glenfinnan

Castle Tioram

Ardnamurchan

Strontian

0 10 20 30 40 km

0 10 20 30 miles

North-west Highlands

The evening sun illuminates the waters at Glenelg on the Sound of Sleat, reached by the hairpinned pass of Mam Ratagan

BEYOND THE GREAT GLEN Fault which slashes through Scotland from Loch Linnhe to the Beauly Firth there are land and sea-scapes of mesmerising variety.

In Caithness there is a lowland landscape beyond the Highlands. The Black Isle is rolling farm and forest land. And on the faraway island beaches of Lewis and Harris, white-tipped Atlantic breakers spill onto gold and silver sands from a turquoise sea.

There are spectacular fresh-water lochs like Shiel and Morar, Affric and Maree. And although the almost eccentrically indented west coast twists and turns past holiday villages at Gairloch and Plockton, Arisaig and Ullapool, it is a working coastline too.

Kinlochbervie, for instance, may be the remotest fishing port in mainland Britain, tucked away at the side of a Sutherland sea-loch; but the landings there are worth £10 million per year.

Tens of thousands of acres of magnificent mountain scenery are protected by the Nature Conservancy Council and the National Trust for Scotland. Prehistoric settlements survive as brochs and duns and standing stones. The influence of the Vikings is clear from place-names like Laxford and Lybster, Valtos and Seilebost.

Clan history comes alive in castles like Dunvegan and Eilean Donan. And this is the country where the fugitive Bonnie Prince Charlie was sheltered after the Jacobite cause was finally lost at Culloden.

APPLECROSS
Ross and Cromarty

On the shore of an exposed, west-facing bay looking out to the island hills of Raasay and the Cuillin peaks of Skye, Applecross village is approached from the east by the lonely and imposing Pass of the Cattle. Hairpin bends on the way to the summit at 2053 ft are loomed over by towering cliffs and rock terraces.

From the north, another single-track road offers spreading views over old crofting settlements to Raasay and its satellite island of Rona.

Southwards, scattered hamlets are beautifully situated at the edge of rocky bays. An intriguing footpath leads through a fringe of woodland to the old village of Coillegillie, a less familiar viewpoint across the Inner Sound to Raasay and Skye.

THE PASS OF THE CATTLE leaves the A896 north of Kishorn; the North Applecross road leaves it south of Shieldaig.

ARDNAMURCHAN
Lochaber

This long and hilly peninsula, mostly occupied by sheep farms and deer forests, ends at mainland Britain's 'farthest west'. The lighthouse on Ardnamurchan Point provides a series of stunning Hebridean views.

Beside the narrow south-coast road, otters frisk in the rocky bays and seals bob up offshore. Minor roads turn north towards the sandy beaches at Sanna, Portuairk and Kilmory.

Near the village of Kilchoan, the ancient monument of Mingary Castle stands on a bluff above the sea. It was in this fortress of the MacIans of Ardnamurchan, in the 1490s, that James IV received the chiefs of the Hebri-

dean clans when, after years of rebellion and punitive expeditions, they were finally forced to acknowledge their allegiance to the Crown.

B8007, the road through Ardnamurchan, turns off the A861 at Salen.

ARISAIG
Lochaber

At the head of Loch nan Ceall, where a flurry of reefs and skerries almost blocks the way to the open sea, Arisaig is famous for its island views, to the abrupt silhouette of Eigg and the grander mountains of Rum and Skye.

There are pleasant walks and drives: for instance, past Camas an-T Salainn — Salt Bay — where stores for the village used to be landed from a beached supply ship.

South-east of Arisaig is Loch nan Uamh. Bonnie Prince Charlie landed here to start the 1745 Jacobite Rising, intended to put his father on the British throne. And this is where, at a place marked by a memorial cairn the dispirited Prince sailed away in September 1746, the last glimmer of hope for a Stuart restoration snuffed out for ever.

ARISAIG is on the A830, 38 miles west of Fort William.

BEINN EIGHE
Ross and Cromarty

Established in 1951, Britain's first National Nature Reserve includes several summits of the Beinn Eighe range and an important fragment of the old Caledonian Pine Forest.

A visitor centre explains the geology and wildlife of the area. There are red and roe deer on the reserve, as well as pine martens and occasional wildcats.

The mountainous Beinn Eighe National Nature Reserve is rich in wildlife

Two nature trails start from a lochside birchwood. The one-mile trail reaches 356 ft, with superb views to the beautifully proportioned peak of Slioch — the Spearhead — across Loch Maree, and to the site of a 17th-century charcoal ironworks.

The four-mile Mountain Trail is a stiffer climb. In clear weather, more than 30 major summits can be identified from its 1800-ft viewpoint.

🚗 *THE BEINN EIGHE reserve visitor centre is at Aultroy, on the A832 half a mile north-west of Kinlochewe.*

BLACK ISLE
Ross and Cromarty

Neither black nor an island, this un-dulating peninsula edged in part with precipitous cliffs mixes farmland and forest with old-established coastal towns and villages.

Rosemarkie's Groam House Museum displays an intricately carv-ed 8th-century Pictish stone. Nearby Fortrose, headquarters of a busy sail-ing club, was once the ecclesiastical centre of the province of Ross, and the ruins of its great cathedral still stand.

The two towns are linked — or separated — by a fine sea-shore golf course on Chanonry Point.

Cromarty was the birthplace of the 19th-century stonemason, geologist, journalist, author and editor Hugh Miller, and his cottage home is main-tained as a museum by the National Trust for Scotland.

The Black Isle is well-known for its walks. More than 20 have been laid out, taking in countryside as different as the mudflats of Udale Bay, pine and larch plantations at Blackstand, an old railway line half-lost in beechwoods near Avoch, the Fairy Glen at Rosemarkie, the fossil beds at Eathie where Hugh Miller studied,

A shroud of mystery 4000 years old covers the 14 standing stones at Callanish

and the clifftops of the South Sutor where derelict gun emplacements watch over the entrance to the Cromarty Firth, once an anchorage of the Home Fleet.

🚗 *THE MAIN access to the Black Isle from the south is by the Kessock Bridge, on the A9 bypassing Inverness.*

CALLANISH STANDING STONES
Western Isles

On a promontory overlooking Loch Roag in Lewis, 13 stones, up to 12 ft high, are arranged in a circle around a taller central megalith. An incomplete double avenue extends to the north, while shorter single lines face east and west.

The Callanish stones stand higher than they did before encroaching peat was dug away in the 1850s, as it was from several other circles within a three-mile radius, all around Loch Roag.

Speculation about their likely astronomical purpose continues. They are no longer considered 'false men' turned to stone by some magic spell. But they are still enveloped in a mystery which stretches back something like 4000 years.

🚗 *CALLANISH is on the A858, 15 miles west of Stornoway.*

CASTLE TIORAM
Lochaber

The 13th-century 'dry castle' has an impressive setting, on the summit of a rocky islet in beautiful Loch Moidart, with the larger, wooded Eilean Shona immediately to the north. At low tide, the castle can be approached on foot over a sand and gravel spit.

Tioram was the impregnable

6 **The spectacular Falls of Measach at Corrieshalloch Gorge**

stronghold of the MacDonalds of Clanranald. But in 1715 the clan chief joined the Jacobite Rising and had the castle set in flames so that, if the Jacobites were defeated, it would never fall into the hands of his traditional enemies, the Campbells.

🚗 *CASTLE TIORAM is 3 miles north of Acharacle, reached by a side-road off the A861.*

CLAN DONALD CENTRE
Skye and Lochalsh

The summer car-ferry from Mallaig to Armadale on Skye has its island terminal at Armadale Bay on the Sleat peninsula, less rugged than the mountain country to the north, and often referred to as 'the garden of Skye'.

Overlooking the bay are the wooded grounds of Armadale Castle. The present building was erected in 1815 for the chief of the MacDonalds of Sleat, but the estate is now in the hands of the Clan Donald Lands Trust.

Part of the square-towered Gothic castle, and its restored stables block, house the Clan Donald Centre, with information on all aspects of the history, genealogy, ancestral territory and world-wide connections of Scotland's largest clan.

🚗 *ARMADALE CASTLE is on the A851, 1 mile north of the ferry terminal.*

CORRIESHALLOCH GORGE
Ross and Cromarty

The most spectacular box canyon in the Highlands is on National Trust for Scotland property at Braemore. A mile long and 200 ft deep, the wooded and precipitous gorge is a copybook habitat for ferns, wildflowers and mosses which relish damp and shadowy conditions.

It is fed by the river which tumbles over the plunging Falls of Measach. Both gorge and waterfall can be seen from a viewing platform and from a handsome Victorian suspension footbridge. This was built, almost as a whimsy, by Sir John Fowler, one of the designers of the Forth Bridge, who was also laird of Braemore.

🚗 *CORRIESHALLOCH GORGE is on the A835, 20 miles north-west of Garve.*

DORNOCH
Sutherland

Once the county town of Sutherland and seat of the bishops of Caithness, Dornoch has many historical connections. Its 13th-century cathedral has been remodelled as the parish church. The turreted Bishop's Palace is now a hotel. The Victorian jail is a museum. And there is a memorial stone to Janet Horn, the last witch executed in Scotland after due process of law, in the year 1722.

But Dornoch is also a pre-eminent golfing resort. The Old Course of Royal Dornoch Golf Club is one of the most highly regarded in the world.

It is on splendid links-land turf, bounded by the extensive beaches which stretch for miles, north and west of the hook-shaped Dornoch Point.

🚗 *DORNOCH is on the A949, 11 miles east of Bonar Bridge.*

DUN CARLOWAY
Western Isles

Not far from the standing stones of Callanish in Lewis, the ruined drystone tower of Dun Carloway is a well-preserved example of a broch — a circular, double-walled Iron Age dwelling of something like beehive shape.

Eilean Donan Castle was built to defend western mainland Scotland against the Vikings

sea-birds make their nests.

East of the village at Smoo there is a famous triple-chambered sea-cave. To the north-west, beyond a craft village whose visitor centre displays the work of potters and jewellers, bookbinders and candlemakers, the dune-backed sands of Balnakiel Bay face the highest sea-cliffs in Britain, towards Cape Wrath.

The ruined church of Balnakiel dates from 1619. It was paid for in part by one Donald McLeod, to ensure his burial in hallowed ground, despite the 18 killings on his conscience.

Also commemorated here is the 18th-century Gaelic bard Rob Donn Mackay, who farmed Balnakiel on behalf of his clan chief, Lord Reay.

DURNESS is on the A838, 30 miles west of Tongue.

EILEAN DONAN CASTLE
Skye and Lochalsh

Set in a dramatic situation on a rocky islet at the junction of Loch Duich and Loch Alsh, with tidal waters, mountains and forests all around, Eilean Donan was built about 1230 as part of Alexander II's defence of the western mainland against the Vikings.

Later, it became the property of the Mackenzie Earls of Seaforth. One of them was heavily involved in the half-cocked Jacobite Rising of 1719, when government warships bombarded the fortress into a smouldering ruin.

After a £250,000 restoration, which started in 1912 and finished 20 years later, Eilean Donan is open to the public as a faithful reproduction of the 18th-century castle.

EILEAN DONAN CASTLE is at Dornie on the A87, 8 miles east of Kyle of Lochalsh.

Its hollow walls were immensely strong, and included several rooms and galleries within them. For security, the entrance was kept both low and narrow, so that intruders could approach only one at a time, and at a crouch.

Maintained as an ancient monument since 1887, Dun Carloway is a fine viewpoint over the rumpled country of rock-outcrops and lochans east of Loch Roag.

DUN CARLOWAY is on the A858, 20 miles west of Stornoway.

DURNESS
Sutherland

This crofting settlement among limestone fields alive with summer wildflowers is flanked by sandy beaches and cliffs where thousands of

ELGOL
Skye and Lochalsh

Beginning high up on the peninsula of Strathaird, the scattered crofting village of Elgol sweeps down towards a shingle beach, past one of the most overwhelming viewpoints on Skye — north and north-west over Loch Scavaig to the saw-toothed peaks of the Black Cuillin.

Westwards across the sea-loch is the island of Soay, where Gavin Maxwell ran a shark fishery — and wrote *Harpoon at a Venture* — before becoming involved with otters and starting a series of best-sellers with *Ring of Bright Water*.

On the roadless coast south of Elgol is the cave where Bonnie Prince Charlie hid, in July 1746, before being rowed in an open boat across the 18 miles to the mainland near Mallaig, on a night of storm-force winds and rain-lashed seas.

ELGOL is on the A881, 14 miles south-west of Broadford.

GAIRLOCH
Ross and Cromarty

Golden sands, sea-angling, trout-fishing in hill and moorland lochs, small-boat sailing, and golf on a coastal course where a despairing glance after a duffed shot may give a consoling sight of the mountain peaks of Torridon — this is the mixture at Gairloch, a holiday resort and at the same time a fishing port with its own small but active harbour.

On the very attractive southern shore of Loch Gairloch there are wooded and deeply-indented bays, before the road follows the coast round past the windblown sands of Opinan to a panoramic viewpoint over Skye and Applecross, above yet another beach at Red Point.

Gairloch Heritage Museum displays farming, fishing and household appliances, to give a fine impression of a West Highland way of life in generations not long gone by.

GAIRLOCH is on the A832, 44 miles west of Garve.

GLEN AFFRIC
Inverness

Once on the route of the great cattle-drives from Skye, Glen Affric owes much of its present appearance to foresters and hydro-electric engineers.

There are modern spruce plantations on most of the hillsides, but an area of the old Caledonian Pine Forest is encouraged to regenerate. And although Loch Affric itself and the lower Loch Benevean feed the hydro-electric power station at Fasnakyle, this activity is very unobtrusive.

Forest walks lead to the Dog Falls in the Affric gorge, and through pine and birchwoods above the river which joins the lochs. One footpath here leads to an impressive viewpoint over the whole lovely glen, the forests and the deer-stalking mountainsides.

THE ROAD to Glen Affric starts at Cannich on the A831. 17 miles south-west of Beauly.

GLENELG
Skye and Lochalsh

Reached by the hairpinned pass of Mam Ratagan, Glenelg is a village on the Sound of Sleat, linked by a summer car-ferry with Kylerhea on Skye.

Near the shore is the substantial ruin of the army barracks erected after the abortive Jacobite Rising of 1719. A largely ineffective garrison was stationed here until the 1770s.

Many of the building stones for the barracks were pilfered from two Pic-tish brochs in nearby Glen Beag, but Dun Telve in particular remains an impressive sight.

Southwards, the road skirts a forest plantation above Sandaig — Gavin Maxwell's 'Camusfearna' — on the way to the even remoter villages of Arnisdale and Corran, facing the forbidding mountain country known as the Rough Bounds of Knoydart across Loch Hourn.

THE MAM RATAGAN road starts at Shiel Bridge on the A87.

GLENFINNAN
Lochaber

On a truly dramatic site, silhouetted against the towering mountains which stretch away down Loch Shiel, the tall Glenfinnan monument is where, in August 1745, Prince Charles Edward Stuart ordered his standard raised — the opening act of the final Jacobite Rising.

The battlemented stone tower was built in 1815 by MacDonald of Glenaladale, one of whose predecessors had been the Prince's host. Beside it is a white rose bush, originally a sprig of the very same bush from which Charles plucked his 'white cockade' — the Jacobite emblem.

The monument is owned by the National Trust for Scotland, whose visitor centre outlines the history of the Rising and the activities of the fighting clans.

GLENFINNAN is on the A830, 17 miles west of Fort William.

GOLSPIE
Sutherland

This trim little town grew up from a handful of turfed huts when tenants evicted from their inland holdings in the Sutherland clearances of the early 19th century came to settle by the sea.

Ironically, Golspie is dominated, from the summit of Ben Bhraggie, by a giant statue of the 1st Duke of Sutherland, in whose name the clearances were made. The Sutherlands' ornate Dunrobin Castle is just north of the village.

St Andrew's church of 1619 has a notable 'laird's loft' for the landowning family. There are attractive walks in the gorge of the Golspie Burn and through hillside pinewoods.

A long sandy beach stretches in front of a testing links golf course. And beyond it, hidden behind grassy bankings, is a first-class kart-racing circuit.

GOLSPIE is on the A9, 22 miles north-east of Bonar Bridge.

HARRIS BEACHES
Western Isles

Although the east coast of Harris is a series of rocky bays, the west coast has a succession of some of the finest beaches in Europe. At Luskentyre by the mouth of the Laxford River, Seilebost, Nisabost, Traigh Iar — the 'west beach' — and Scarista, breakers roll in from the Atlantic, over beaches backed by dunes and grassy banks.

The extensive sands of Scarista have been used as a landing ground by light planes, and the smooth turf behind them is where the annual Harris sheep-dog trials are held. More peacefully, most of the beaches are within strolling distance of ancient chambered cairns and standing stones.

THE HARRIS BEACHES are beside the A859 Tarbert to Leverburgh road.

The Glenfinnan Monument occupies a breathtaking lochside site where the Stuart standard was raised in 1745 9

INVEREWE GARDEN
Ross and Cromarty

In 1862, when Osgood Mackenzie became the owner of this bare sandstone peninsula at the head of the Loch Ewe, there was not only an almost complete absence of plant-life apart from heather and crowberries, but also an almost complete absence of soil.

He imported tons of it, planted pine-tree windbreaks and in the fullness of time created a splendid garden of exotic plants, shrubs and trees, sheltered from the salt-laden winds.

Now owned by the National Trust for Scotland, the 26 acres of Inverewe house something like 2500 different species — a subtropical garden level in latitude with Greenland.

INVEREWE GARDEN is on the A832, half a mile north of Poolewe.

INVERPOLLY
Ross and Cromarty

This is one of the largest National Nature Reserves in Britain — more than 26,000 acres, all but uninhabited, of primeval mountains, remote lochs with birch-studded islands, tumbling rivers and a stretch of sea-coast at Enard Bay.

The highest peak is Cul Mor at 2876 ft, but the most bizarre — seen clearly from the road along Loch Lurgainn on the south side of the reserve — is Stac Polly, with a fantastic series of towers, pinnacles and rock-flakes forming its summit ridge.

The main public access to the reserve is at Knockan on the eastern boundary. There is a visitor centre and a fascinating waymarked trail which points out the geological curiosities of the Knockan Cliff.

KNOCKAN is on the A835, 11 miles north of Ullapool.

10

Angling in Scotland

A glance at even a small-scale map of the North-west Highlands and the Western Isles makes it clear why this is such a fine area for trout and salmon anglers. There are innumerable major lochs and rivers, burns and scattered hill lochans.

Parts of islands like North Uist and Benbecula, for example, seem to be almost as much water as land. On Lewis, fishing estates like Grimersta and Garynahine include complete river systems and chains of lochs.

On the mainland, Loch Maree is not only spectacularly beautiful, with its surrounding mountains and scatter of wooded islands; it is also world-famous for its sea-trout.

Flowing north into the Pentland Firth there are substantial salmon rivers like the Halladale and the Thurso. Others — like the Helmsdale, where the first salmon of the year in Scotland is often landed — flow into the Moray Firth.

In the far north, some places on the map — like Forsinard and Altnaharra — have angling hotels as very nearly the main reason for being there at all.

Some fishing waters are

controlled by private estates or hotels — Scourie Hotel in Sutherland has rights on more than 200 lochs; some by public bodies like the Forestry Commission; and others by

angling associations.

The finances of the sport are equally varied. Many hotels offer their guests fishing at no extra charge; and bank fishing on some lochs is available for as little as £1 per rod per day.

But there are some much more rarefied estates, on which the cost of a single week's salmon fishing and accommodation can be over £1000 — for an acceptable individual prepared to wait anything up to two years for the privilege.

Left Young anglers at Stornoway
Below Fishing fleet in the harbour at Kyle of Lochalsh

JOHN O'GROATS
Caithness

John o'Groats — named after the 15th-century ferryman Jan de Groot — is often publicised as the most northerly point on the British mainland, although that superlative really belongs to Dunnet Head, a few miles

away along the northern coast.

North of the village itself, the hotel and pier at the very end of the road have a fine view to the deserted island of Stroma and, beyond it, to Orkney. A summer-time ferry runs to Burwick on the Orkney island of South Ronaldsay. Boats also sail along the coast past the precipitous rocky inlets

called geos to Duncansby Head, which with its lighthouse can also be reached by car. But the boats continue southwards 'round the corner' past the sea-bird colonies on the cliffs to where jagged sandstone stacks rise offshore.

JOHN O'GROATS is on the A9, 14 miles north of Wick.

Stac Polly seen across Loch Lurgainn in the stunning Inverpolly Nature Reserve

KYLE OF SUTHERLAND
Sutherland

The hillsides around this narrow tidal waterway fed by the Rivers Oykel and Shin are clothed in conifer plantations. One forest walk goes through pine, spruce and larch at Carbisdale, the only castle built in Britain this century. Another makes for the salmon-leap waterfalls in the gorge of the Shin.

There are old watermills in the area, Victorian ice-houses built to ease the transport of salmon, and many prehistoric sites.

Lairg, north of the Falls of Shin, is a famous livestock trading centre. In August it hosts the biggest one-day sheep sale in Europe.

KYLE OF SUTHERLAND is on the A836, immediately north-west of Bonar Bridge.

LEVERBURGH
Western Isles

Until 1923 this village on the Sound of Harris was known as Obbe — from the Gaelic word *ob*, which indicated the tidal creek immediately back from the shore.

In that year the millionaire industrialist Lord Leverhulme decided to transform Obbe into a major Hebridean fishing port, re-naming it after himself.

The great project to build new roads and houses, a modern pier and processing sheds was put under way; but Leverhulme died in 1925 and the whole scheme was abandoned.

Now the main attraction for visitors to Leverburgh is a modern craft centre with a museum which tells the story of a more enduring local industry — Harris tweed.

LEVERBURGH is on the A859, 19 miles south-west of Tarbert.

KILMUIR
Skye and Lochalsh

The old churchyard at Kilmuir in the north of Skye, with its extensive seaward views to the Western Isles, is a place of pilgrimage for people from all over the world. They come to visit the grave, marked by a stately Celtic cross, of Flora MacDonald, who, with the connivance of her father — an army officer but also a Jacobite sympathiser — arranged the famous escape of Bonnie Prince Charlie from the island of Benbecula, when troops were closing in on his hiding place. This is the story told in the famous *Skye Boat Song*.

Also at Kilmuir, a group of old thatched houses is now a folk museum — one is a typical croft cottage, another a weaving shed, the third displays a collection of documents, while the fourth is laid out as a blacksmith's forge.

KILMUIR is on the A855, 6 miles north of Uig.

LOCHALSH WOODLAND GARDEN
Skye and Lochalsh

Planted around 1890, Lochalsh House grounds are maintained by the National Trust for Scotland as a specialised woodland garden. The original tree cover of beech and oak, larch and several kinds of pine combines with the garden's location above a rocky shore to provide habitats for a great variety of birds.

Winding footpaths meander through the woodlands, which also contain exotic shrubs from Asia and the Pacific, and are currently being redeveloped.

A visitor centre in the old coach house stands close to a viewpoint above the coastline, looking through the narrows of the Sound of Sleat.

LOCHALSH WOODLAND GARDEN is off the A87, 3 miles east of Kyle of Lochalsh.

LYBSTER
Caithness

Viking settlers gave this substantial Caithness village its name — 'the homestead on the hill'. From an early 19th-century coaching inn, a side-road dips down to an extensive harbour, separate from the village itself, in a fold of the rumpled coastline at the mouth of the Reisgill Burn.

Last century, Lybster was for a time the third biggest fishing port in Scotland. It supported a thriving community of fishermen, fish-curers, coopers and general labourers.

When the herring shoals went farther north, business slumped dramatically. But the harbour has recently been improved again, and Lybster still maintains its own small fishing fleet.

LYBSTER is on the A9, 13 miles south of Wick.

Mallaig's crowded waters bob with fishing boats and ferries jostling to take visitors to the Isles

Mallaig kippers — a local delicacy

MALLAIG
Lochaber

The opening in 1901 of the Mallaig extension of the West Highland Railway transformed this previously tiny hamlet on a rocky coast into a ferry terminal and busy fishing port.

A hill road progresses to Mallaigvaig, providing an eagle's-eye view across the Sound of Sleat to Skye. And a rougher continuation opens up to walkers the rarely-seen vista of the hill-country of Knoydart across the mouth of Loch Nevis.

Major ferry destinations from Mallaig include Armadale on Skye; the islands of Rum, Eigg, Muck and Canna; and — through the Sound of Sleat — Kyle of Lochalsh.

Small boats operate regular but occasional services to Inverie and Tarbet, places with no road connections on the mountainous Loch Nevis shores.

🚗 *MALLAIG is on the A830, 46 miles west of Fort William.*

MELLON UDRIGLE
Ross and Cromarty

This hamlet on an inlet of Gruinard Bay has a curiously mixed Gaelic and Norse name, meaning 'Idrigill's little hill'. Its beautiful silver beach is backed by dunes which were badly threatened by erosion until taken in hand

Morar's dazzling white sands and freshwater loch attract many visitors

— as part of a national environmental project of the 1970s — by the children of a Midlothian school.

Mellon Udrigle, with a handful of cottages looking across shell-sand turf and a burn trickling along the edge of the sands, is one of the pleasantest picnic places in Wester Ross, facing the outstanding peaks of Coigach beyond the scattering of islands in the mouth of Loch Broom.

🚗 *MELLON UDRIGLE is 3 miles north of Laide on the A832.*

MORAR
Lochaber

The village of Morar backs onto a curving estuary with magnificent white sands rising on both sides. A remarkably short stretch of non-tidal river links it with the freshwater Loch Morar, which is 12 miles long, rarely more than a mile and a half wide, and by any standard one of the most beautiful lochs in Scotland.

At the west end there is a cluster of attractively wooded islands. An exhilarating footpath follows the north shore to Swordale, off which phenomenal soundings of more than 1000 ft have been recorded. And there have been, as at Loch Ness, persistent stories of some unidentified creature occasionally surfacing from those almost impenetrable depths.

🚗 *MORAR is on the A830, 3 miles south of Mallaig.*

PLOCKTON
Ross and Cromarty

This spectacularly located village spreads along a main bay and some narrower rocky inlets on the shore of Loch Carron, a popular small-boat sailing ground.

Plockton was settled by early 19th-century smallholders evicted from the hill grazings which were then more profitably rented out to sheep-farmers. After a time as a boat

building centre, it is now a highly regarded holiday resort.

One very pleasant walk is through the woodland fringe around the head of the village bay, towards the Victorian Duncraig Castle with its towering backdrop of rugged crags and buttresses. Another is along the edge of the hill above Harbour Street, with the back gardens of the houses falling steeply away below.

🚗 *PLOCKTON is 7 miles northeast of Kyle of Lochalsh.*

PORTREE
Skye and Lochalsh

Although it is principally the administrative, business and shopping centre of Skye, Portree also has a broad harbour area. Overlooked by tiers of colour-washed houses, shops and hotels, the harbour is only a tiny part of a larger sea-loch dominated by soaring outer cliffs.

Immediately above the fishing boat

13

quay, wooded crags rise to a level sports field where the Skye Games are held every summer.

Bonnie Prince Charlie and Flora MacDonald parted for the last time in Portree, but the inn where they said goodbye has been replaced by a modern hotel.

In fact, the oldest occupied building in Portree dates only from 1810 — Meall House, the tourist information centre, which originally served as the jail!

 PORTREE is on the A856, 35 miles from the ferry terminal at Kyleakin.

QUIRAING
Skye and Lochalsh

Running for miles north of Portree, and forming the central spine of the huge Trotternish peninsula, is an escarpment of basalt cliffs. Here and there, ancient landslips have eroded into a series of separated rock pinnacles and grass-topped towers.

One of the most majestic of these areas, reached by a hairpinned minor road which clambers up the escarpment itself, is the Quiraing, which can be explored by an access path along the foot of cliffs and scree-runs.

It is not only a place of outstanding scenery and widespread views, but also a natural garden of rare alpine flowers.

 THE QUIRAING is on the minor road between Staffin and Uig.

RAASAY
Skye and Lochalsh

This long, narrow, green and remarkably varied island has all kinds of hill, moorland and forest walks with close-up views to the mountains of Skye and Applecross.

Ruined Brochel Castle, in golden eagle country on the north-east coast, was the stronghold of the MacLeod lairds until they moved to Raasay House, where Dr Johnson was famously entertained in 1773. Fearns on the south-east coast is at the start of a walk by birchwoods to the fine waterfall at Hallaig.

Derelict remains survive of the ironstone mine workings of World War I. The incongruous 'workers-row' village of Inverarish was built — with armed sentry-posts — for the German prisoners who made up most of the labour force.

 THE CAR-FERRY terminal for Raasay is at Sconser on Skye, on the A850, 12 miles south of Portree.

RODEL
Western Isles

At the south-eastern tip of Harris, this village is overlooked by the most notable church in the Hebrides. St Clement's, with its square, battlemented tower, was built in 1528 by Alexander MacLeod of Dunvegan, 8th chief of the clan. His lavishly carved tomb is the main feature of a carefully preserved ancient monument.

The MacLeods' hereditary standard-bearers used to be buried here too — all in the same stone coffin in the chancel. Whenever one of them was laid to rest, his predecessor's bones were still there, and had to be pushed down through a grating to make way for the new arrival.

 RODEL is on the A859, 3 miles south-east of Leverburgh.

STRATHPEFFER
Ross and Cromarty

In Victorian and Edwardian times, this dignified village of stone-built villas, boarding-houses and hotels — all in streets which to this day have no names — was the most northerly

One of Scotland's finest mountains, the quartzite topped Liathach ridge is part of the Torridon estate

spa in Britain. A fashionable clientèle came to 'take the waters' of its sulphur and chalybeate springs, or recline in all manner of therapeutic baths.

All that has passed, but Strathpeffer is still very much a holiday resort, offering golf, angling, hill and woodland walks.

A large Bavarian-style hotel overlooks the attractive village square. The pump room and spa pavilion have been restored, and although the Strathpeffer branch line is long since closed, the Highland Railway station of 1885, with its elegant glass canopy, has been turned into a craft and visitor centre.

STRATHPEFFER *is on the A834, 4 miles west of Dingwall.*

STRONTIAN
Lochaber

This modern village and the older crofting settlements in the valley of the Strontian River are all on Crown property, bought in 1920 to guarantee land to returned ex-servicemen.

North-east of the village, the Strontian Glen nature trail passes through an oakwood reserve to a high moorland around old lead mines, worked at intervals since 1722.

Other disused mines can be seen from the narrow and twisting hill road which goes over a pass with wide-ranging views of the forests and mountainsides around Loch Shiel, to the remote village, built by the Forestry Commission, at Polloch.

STRONTIAN *is on the A861, 14 miles west of Corran Ferry.*

TORRIDON
Ross and Cromarty

Along the north side of Glen Torridon and the sea-loch to the west, the National Trust for Scotland's 16,000-acre estate of the same name includes all seven summits of the quartzite-topped Liathach ridge — a riot of steep rock terraces, skyline pinnacles and menacing screes — and the sandstone peaks of Beinn Alligin, soaring up from the shore of Upper Loch Torridon.

There are beautifully located villages along the lochside: Torridon itself, beyond the NTS visitor centre and red-deer museum; Alligin and Wester Alligin with their majestic views across the water to Beinn Shieldaig and Beinn Damh; and Diabaig, where the road plunges down to a bay circled by a wild rocky amphitheatre.

THE TORRIDON *road turns off the A896, 10 miles south-west of Kinlochewe.*

ULLAPOOL
Ross and Cromarty

Curiously located where a triangle of level ground sweeps out into Loch Broom from an otherwise hilly coast, Ullapool was one of the settlements created in the 1780s by the British Fisheries Society.

The modern village, where whitewashed hotels, shops and houses face an inner bay, still earns much of its living, directly or indirectly, from the sea. It is the car-ferry port for Stornoway in Lewis; and freezer ships from Eastern Europe buy up the catches of fishing boats operating in the Minch.

Old-style Ullapool fishing is recalled in the excellent Loch Broom Museum, housed in one of the town's original buildings.

There is recreational sailing here too, as well as sea-angling and cruises to sea-bird and seal colonies. Nearby, too, is the Inverpolly Nature Reserve.

ULLAPOOL *is on the A835, 32 miles north-west of Garve.*

Ullapool is a popular resort and traditional fishing port, famous for white fish. It also attracts sea anglers

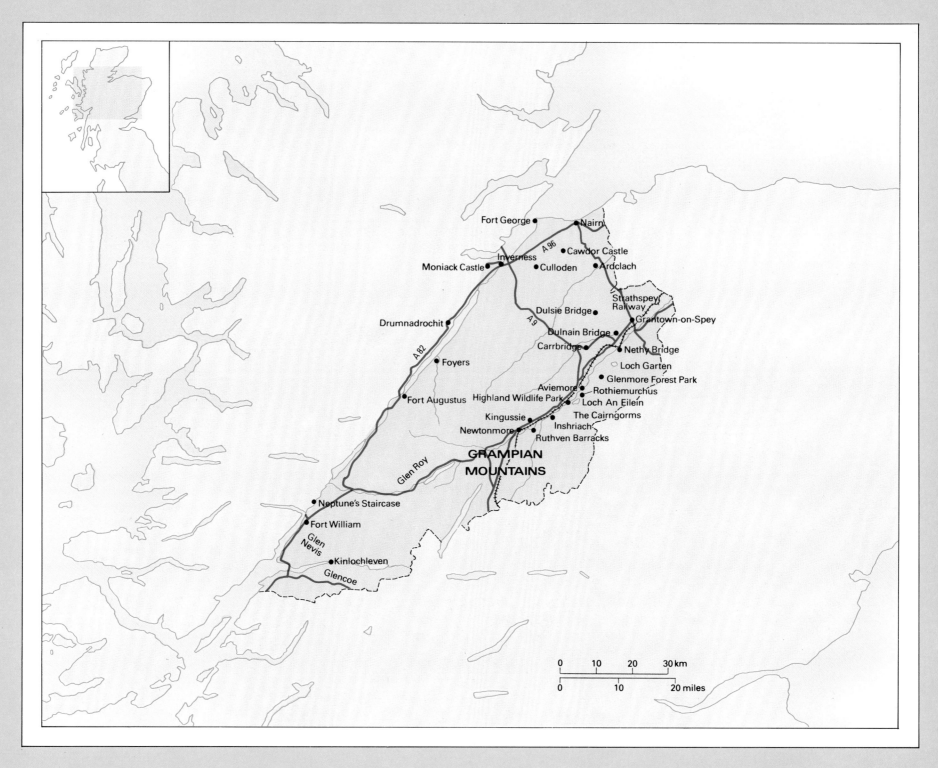

Fort George
Nairn
Inverness
A 96
Cawdor Castle
Moniack Castle
Culloden
Ardclach
Strathspey Railway
Dulsie Bridge
Grantown-on-Spey
Drumnadrochit
A 9
Dulnain Bridge
Carrbridge
Nethy Bridge
A 82
Foyers
Loch Garten
Glenmore Forest Park
Aviemore
Rothiemurchus
Highland Wildlife Park
Loch An Eilein
Fort Augustus
Kingussie
The Cairngorms
Inshriach
Newtonmore
Ruthven Barracks
GRAMPIAN
MOUNTAINS
Glen Roy
Neptune's Staircase
Fort William
Glen
Nevis
Kinlochleven
Glencoe

0	10	20	30 km
0	10		20 miles

Great Glen & Speyside

One of Scotland's best-known historic sites, Glencoe is a tremendous deep-cut glen amid glorious mountain scenery. Once the scene of a hideous massacre, the glen is now a place of tranquillity

MOUNTAINS AND FORESTS, together with lochs and river valleys following the general north-east/south-west lie of the land, make up this varied and beautiful area of the Central Highlands — which has coastal lowlands around Nairn and Inverness.

The Great Glen can be traced almost ruler-straight on any map of Scotland. Britain's highest mountains are here — Ben Nevis and the Cairngorms. And in the middle valley of the Spey there is a busy all-year-round holiday area where resort attractions are only a few minutes away from birch and pinewood walks, nature trails, castles, fortresses and faint reminders of old Highland industries long since stilled.

There are many unexpected places, like the little upland 'lake district'

among the grass and heather moors south of Inverness; the road ablaze with golden flowers of broom and gorse that leads to Dores; the low-key road junction in Fort William which points the way to the majestic Nevis gorge; and the lonely glen where an eerie landscape once believed to be the work of giants finally revealed its secrets to the 19th-century eye of science.

In the high Cairngorms there are nesting birds known to lowland ornithologists only from illustrations in books. And ospreys, which shunned Scotland for many of their generations, are re-establishing themselves in the Highlands from an original single nest in the Abernethy pine forest.

The Aviemore ski centre is popular all year round as both expert skiers and beginners can take advantage of the dry practice slopes

ARDCLACH
Nairn

This is a very attractive parish of farm and forest land split by the wandering course of the River Findhorn. The old church of 1626 is oddly located, on a fan of low-lying ground where hills rise from a sweeping bend on the river.

In the early years, that caused a problem, because the sound of the church bell — not just a call to Sunday service, but also the traditional warning that cattle-raiders had been seen — carried only a short distance. So a separate bell tower was built on the hillside above.

Later, the bell tower was where parishioners who had offended against church rules were sometimes detained. It is now an ancient monument.

ARDCLACH is reached by a side-road off the A939, 1½ miles north of Ferness.

AVIEMORE
Badenoch and Strathspey

In the 18th century, Aviemore was a tiny settlement round an inn on the military road through the Spey Valley. The railway arrived in mid-Victorian times, and a modest village-style holiday resort developed.

Then in 1966 the multi-million pound Aviemore Centre was opened, swamping the older village with a modern resort of hotels, chalets, restaurants, shops, a theatre, cinema, swimming pool, ice rink, sauna and dry ski slope.

Aviemore is an all-year-round resort, since it is also the main accommodation centre for the Cairngorm ski slopes, on the mountains which soar up from the pine forests across the Spey and provide it with a memorable eastward view.

While the open Cairngorm slopes are used for the downhill runs, many of the forest tracks are signposted for cross-country skiers.

Immediately above Aviemore, peregrine falcons nest on the rock-face of Craigellachie. There is another Craigellachie more than 30 miles away in the lower course of the Spey. The two cliffs marked the eastern and western limits of the territory of Clan Grant, who used 'Stand fast, Craigellachie!' as their battle-cry.

A nature trail is laid out through the Craigellachie birchwoods, where the tiny Loch Puladdern is stocked with brown and rainbow trout.

AVIEMORE is on the A9, 30 miles south-east of Inverness.

CARRBRIDGE
Badenoch and Strathspey

Now bypassed by the main Aviemore to Inverness road, this is a village holiday resort with a golf course, pony-trekking and a substantial interest in the Cairngorm ski-ing.

Built in 1717, the original Bridge of Carr survives as a beautifully proportioned arch across the River Dulnain.

The imaginative Landmark Visitor Centre is set in 30 acres of old-established pine forest. It has a multi-screen audio-visual show in a modern theatre overlooking a lochan.

Outside in the pinewoods, other attractions include an adventure playground and mile-long woodland maze, a contemporary sculpture park, a conventional nature trail and another on stilts at tree-top level, from which roe deer, red squirrels,

A solitary cairn at windswept Culloden stands as an eerie reminder of the last bloody battle for supremacy fought on British soil

goldcrests and crossbills can sometimes be seen.

🚗 *CARRBRIDGE is on the B9150, 6 miles north of Aviemore.*

CAWDOR CASTLE
Nairn

Not simply a museum-piece, but also the home of the Earl of Cawdor, this splendid castle with its crow-stepped gables and turreted central keep stands among lawns and gardens, backed by mellow oak and beechwoods cut by tumbling burns.

In Shakespeare's play, Macbeth was Thane of Cawdor, and his castle was where King Duncan was murdered. But the present Cawdor Castle post-dates *Macbeth* by many generations: the keep is known to have been built in 1454.

However, part of the castle is cer-

tainly older, and there is a family tradition that the builder was instructed in a dream to place it beside a hawthorn tree.

This sounds a typical legendary tale; except that, as well as the elegant sitting rooms, the kitchens and the dungeons shown to the public, there is also, deep in the heart of the castle, a tiny chamber where, even to this day, a tiny fragment of an ancient and dessicated hawthorn can still be seen.

🚗 *CAWDOR is on the B9090, 5 miles south-west of Nairn.*

CULLODEN
Inverness

The last great pitched battle on British soil was fought on 16 April 1746, when the Duke of Cumberland's government army

routed the Jacobite forces on Culloden Moor.

From the outnumbered Jacobites' point of view, the place, the time and the set-piece style of the battle could not have been more ineptly chosen.

Open moorland facing a better-equipped enemy was hopeless terrain for the Highlanders' favourite tactic of a fearsome, claymores-drawn charge; their attack was intended to be at night, but was delayed so long that it had to be postponed till daylight; once the battle started, Cumberland's far superior artillery poured withering cannon and mortar fire on the opposing ranks; he also had the advantage in cavalry; when the Jacobites finally charged, the movement was unco-ordinated, and the well-trained government troops, including those from non-Jacobite Scottish regiments, held their line.

Prince Charles, who had taken bad advice, retreated from the field. But Cumberland, son of King George II against whom the Rising was directed, started a reign of terror.

The murders and lootings which followed Culloden explain why, although he was greeted back in London with Handel's specially-composed *Hail, the Conquering Hero Comes*, he is still known in many parts of Scotland as 'the Butcher'.

The battlefield is now owned by the National Trust for Scotland. A visitor centre explains the course of the whole 'Forty-Five Rising. There are memorials and clan burial grounds. And the modern road cuts across the opposing armies' lines, as they were on the day when the Highlands changed for ever.

🚗 *CULLODEN MOOR is on the B9006, 4 miles east of Inverness.*

DRUMNADROCHIT
Inverness

Lying back from Urquhart Bay on Loch Ness, this is a low-set village with forest plantations, farms and isolated houses climbing the steep hillside to the north.

Urquhart Castle, a ruin overlooking the bay, was destroyed after the early Jacobite Rising of 1689. This is where many sightings have been reported of whatever it may be that is called the Loch Ness Monster. The comprehensive Loch Ness Monster Exhibition, with photographic, sonar and other records, is in the village.

Beside the main road south is a memorial to John Cobb, who was the holder of the world land speed record in 1952, when he was killed on Loch Ness trying to set a new water speed record in his boat *Crusader*.

🚗 *DRUMNADROCHIT is on the A82, 14 miles south of Inverness.*

DULNAIN BRIDGE
Badenoch and Strathspey

About a mile upstream from where the River Dulnain meets the Spey, overlooked by woodlands and hill farms, this 18th-century bridge and the village clustered round it used to mark the boundary between the counties of Inverness and Moray.

Dulnain Bridge is a small but individual holiday resort. Many visitors come for the Dulnain's 12 miles of salmon and trout-fishing.

On the south side of the bridge, a side-road runs through the spread-out crofting settlement of Skye of Curr, where the Speyside Heather Garden Centre displays more than 200 cultivated varieties of Scotland's best-known wildflower.

🚗 *DULNAIN BRIDGE is on the A95, 3 miles south-west of Grantown-on-Spey.*

DULSIE BRIDGE
Nairn

The military road of the 1750s from Deeside to Fort George on the Moray Firth was designed by Major Caulfield, successor to General Wade as the great road-builder in the Highlands. Caulfield was responsible for several routes — including this one — mistakenly marked on the map as 'Wade roads'.

When it came to crossing the River Findhorn at Dulsie, Caulfield encountered a ravine with rock pools and birchwoods. He built a sturdy but picturesque little high-level bridge which survives to the present day.

Nearby, a side-road follows the Findhorn upstream towards the heavily eroded valley, flanked by heathery grouse moors.

🚗 *DULSIE BRIDGE is reached from a crossroads on the B9007, 14 miles north of Carrbridge.*

FORT AUGUSTUS
Inverness

This forestry, angling and sailing centre at the head of Loch Ness is on the Great Glen Fault, which provides the deep trough-like structure of Loch Ness and also accommodates the Caledonian Canal. A Great Glen Exhibition has been established at the main-road canal bridge.

St Benedict's Abbey, open to visitors, stands in beautifully wooded grounds, between the canal and the River Tarff. The original building here was the Hanoverian fort which gave the village its name. It remained in government hands until 1867. Nine years later it was gifted to the Benedictine Order.

Within four more years a monastery, chapel, boarding school and guesthouse had been created from renovated military buildings. The cloisters were new, of fine grey granite with decorated Gothic windows overlooking the lawn which covers the original flagstone courtyard of the fort.

The Abbey remains one of the finest groups of integrated buildings in the Highlands.

🚗 *FORT AUGUSTUS is on the A82, 33 miles north of Fort William.*

FORT GEORGE
Inverness

In the aftermath of Culloden, the government constructed one of the most formidable 18th-century fortresses in Europe on a promontory which matches Chanonry Point in the Black Isle to form the narrows of the Moray Firth.

Fort George is the biggest fort in Britain, but by the time it was completed in the 1760s there was no longer any Jacobite threat to test its

Ben Nevis rises majestically beyond the ruins of Inverlochy Castle

complex landward defences or the gun emplacements on its massive bastions.

In fact, Fort George has never heard a shot fired in anger, but it is still garrisoned. The parts classified as an ancient monument are open to the public, as is the regimental museum of the Queen's Own Highlanders, and there are impressive views from the mile-long rampart walk, especially to the cliffs of the Black Isle.

FORT GEORGE is on the B9006, 8 miles west of Nairn.

FORT WILLIAM
Lochaber

Built on a spectacular site — partly on a hillside rising directly from Loch Linnhe, and partly on flatter ground at the mouth of the River Lochy with the great bulk of Ben Nevis looming behind — Fort William is the business and communications centre of Lochaber.

The fort which gave it its English name — and its Gaelic name, which means 'the garrison' — was built in 1690 during the reign of William III. Almost all trace of it was swept away in Victorian times. An older fortress which survives as an ancient monument is the 13th-century Inverlochy Castle.

Several Jacobite relics are displayed in the West Highland Museum, including a famous 'secret portrait' of Bonnie Prince Charlie. This is a tray painted with apparently random coloured daubs. But when a reflecting cylinder is put in place on it, a portrait of the Prince suddenly appears.

FORT WILLIAM is on the A82, south of its junction with the A830 Mallaig road.

FOYERS
Inverness

This attractively suited village, built on a Wade road of the 1730s, is on a steeply-rising forested hillside above Loch Ness. Plunging down a dramatic rocky gorge, the Falls of Foyers were harnessed in the 1890s to

The tranquil atmosphere of St Benedict's Abbey is well-preserved and enjoyed by many visitors to Fort Augustus

The Cairngorms

Although they extend over both Highland and Grampian Regions, the Cairngorms — for non-climbers — are more easily approached from their western side above the Spey Valley. The 'ski road' from Glenmore climbs high above the tree line, well up the bare hill slopes.

Beyond the final car park there

The spectacular snow-capped peaks and the gentler grassy slopes of the Cairngorm Mountains attract climbers

is the choice of a winding footpath up Coire Cas — the main ski-ing area, where once the spring snows have cleared the ground is seen to be heavily scarred — or by the chairlift to the Ptarmigan Restaurant.

From the Ptarmigan, which is already among the frost-shattered granite rocks characteristic of the Cairngorm plateau, it is only a short walk to the 4084-ft summit of Cairn Gorm itself.

'Plateau' is a fairly mild word for this high-level landscape, the most extensive area of mountains in Britain over 3000 ft; and 'summit' is also misleading, since the actual tops of the Cairngorms have nothing to offer climbers.

The rolling tableland is interrupted by sudden corries gouged out by the last of the glaciers, and it is there that the steepest slopes occur — colossal descents of rock and scree to the glacial lochs far below.

Birds never seen in lowland Britain nest here — ptarmigan, snow bunting and dotterel. Heather fades out by 4000 ft, hardy rushes and grasses take over, and alpine plants are mostly restricted to the corries.

It is important to remember that this *is* the highest mountain plateau in Britain. Even on a fine summer day there is a stiff temperature drop compared with the valleys, and the wind-chill factor must always be taken into account. The plateau is no place for a casual, ill-equipped stroll at any time of year, as walkers have often found to their cost.

provide hydro-electric power for a pioneering aluminium factory built near the lochside.

The factory closed in 1967, although its Victorian buildings remain. But hydro-electricity is still of major importance at Foyers, which is now the site of a pumped-storage generating scheme.

Narrow wooded pathways, and a railed-off belvedere, give excellent views of the falls. There are forest walks to the north. And this is another place where sightings of the Loch Ness Monster have been reported.

FOYERS is on the B852, 11 miles north-east of Fort Augustus.

GLEN NEVIS
Lochaber

In the middle of Fort William, an unobtrusive bridge over the River Nevis marks the entrance to one of the most magnificent mountain scenes in Scotland. The north-bank road leads to the so-called 'tourist path' up Ben Nevis — a real mountain trek to the summit plateau at over 4400 ft, and not to be tackled lightly.

South of the river, another road forms the first section of the 95-mile West Highland Way towards the outskirts of Glasgow; passes Glen Nevis House, the Jacobite headquarters during the siege of Fort William in 1746; crosses the river at the lower Nevis falls and finishes at a car park from which a spectacular footpath continues.

It threads its way to where the mountains jam even closer together to form the precipitous birch and pine-clad slopes of the Nevis gorge. Above the gorge, a waterfall dashes down a hanging valley beside the climbers' hut at Steall.

THE GLEN NEVIS road turns east off the A82 in Fort William.

GLEN ROY
Lochaber

From a Nature Conservancy viewpoint halfway up this narrow valley north of Glen Spean, the famous 'parallel roads' are clearly seen. These wide grassy ledges circle the heathery hillsides at three different levels — about 1149 ft, 1068 ft and 857 ft.

It was only in Victorian times that the puzzle of how they were created was finally solved.

The 'roads' are actually the ancient shorelines of the glacier lake which filled Glen Roy during the Ice Age, and the three levels show how movements of the main glacier in Glen Spean allowed the lake to drop.

GLEN ROY is entered from Roybridge on the A86, 3 miles east of Spean Bridge.

GLENCOE
Lochaber

This tremendous deep-cut glen with its almost overwhelming mountain scenery is well-known to anyone with the faintest interest in Highland history.

The National Trust for Scotland's 14,000-acre Glencoe estate includes most of the south-side peaks and ridges, as well as the northern mountain wall.

In the wooded lower part of the glen there is an NTS visitor centre, a folk museum and a beautiful forest walk to a lochan overlooked by ranks of Corsican pines.

But Glencoe is best remembered for the massacre of February 1692, when a company of government troops billeted on the MacDonalds of Glencoe were ordered to wipe out the entire population of the glen.

Because their chief had been delayed in taking the compulsory oath of allegiance to William III, the MacDonalds could be technically regarded as rebels.

In fact, thanks partly to veiled warnings from some of the soldiers, many of them escaped into the snowy mountain passes. But an annual memorial service at the MacDonald

Backpacks and stout hiking boots are essential for those determined to scale the heights of Glencoe

The indoor collection at Kingussie Folk Museum includes this scene of a blacksmith at work

monument beside the Bridge of Coe is only one long-standing reminder of an offence that shocked the country — the execrated crime of 'murder under trust'.

GLENCOE is on the A82, 15 miles south of Fort William.

GLENMORE FOREST PARK
Badenoch and Strathspey

Bought by the Forestry Commission in 1923, this one-time estate of the Dukes of Gordon is one of Scotland's most beautifully located forest areas, between the heather-purple corries of the Cairngorms and the River Spey. The plantations are mainly of Scots pine and Sitka spruce, while the park also contains open mountainside.

It begins with plantations round three sides of Loch Morlich, more than 1000 ft above sea level and a popular — if chilly — sailing, canoeing, windsurfing and angling water.

There are waymarked walks in the conifer plantations, more substantial trekking routes on the ridges and through the hill passes.

Glenmore Lodge, at the entrance to the glaciated Pass of Ryvoan, is the National Outdoor Training Centre; courses are run here in outdoor sports and mountain rescue.

Visits can be arranged to the high-level grazings of Scotland's only reindeer herd, established from Lapland stock in 1952.

Lower down, the forest itself is the home of black grouse, capercaillie and the curious crossbill, whose beak is designed to winkle into pine cones for the seeds which are its staple diet.

GLENMORE FOREST PARK is 5 miles east of Aviemore.

GRANTOWN-ON-SPEY
Badenoch and Strathspey

Named after the Grant family who, in the 1760s, began to lease out house-building sites on a barren moorland near their castle, this is a carefully planned little town centred on a handsome square of 18th and 19th-century houses, shops, hotels and public buildings.

Although Grantown had a brief but successful foray into the linen trade, it began to flourish as a holiday resort after the railway came through in the 1860s.

There is excellent salmon and trout fishing on the local beats of the River Spey; a fine golf course, an outdoor curling pond first used in 1865, and other sports facilities; and very pleasant walking on the pine-needled footpaths of the Anagach Wood, the Free Church Wood and the Ladies Garden Wood.

Grantown is also well placed, of course, for the Cairngorm ski slopes.

GRANTOWN-ON-SPEY is on the A95, 14 miles north-east of Aviemore.

HIGHLAND WILDLIFE PARK
Badenoch and Strathspey

Established in 1972 over 250 acres of heathery moorland dotted with birches, in the foothills of the Monadhliath· this park has a collection not only of animals and birds currently living in Scotland in the wild, but also of others whose native strain died out hundreds or even thousands of years ago.

A 200-acre drive-through area is home to red and roe deer, Highland cattle and a herd of bison built up from a few animals sent from a breeding colony in a Polish forest.

There are smaller enclosures for

wildcats, pine martens, foxes, lynx and bears, and the park maintains its own wolf pack.

Birds range from eagles and snowy owls in the collection to snipe and lapwing which come here naturally to nest.

THE HIGHLAND WILDLIFE PARK is on the B9152, 8 miles southwest of Aviemore.

INSHRIACH
Badenoch and Strathspey

Forestry Commission conifer plantations occupy most of the one-time moorland of this small district east of the Spey. A picnic site above the rapids and rock pools of Feshiebridge is the start of a short walk to a viewpoint over the forest towards the Cairngorms.

A mile to the south is the airstrip from which the Cairngorm Gliding Club take advantage of the rising air currents of the mountain edge.

Established in 1938, the Inshriach Nursery attracts visitors from all over the world. It has a collection of more than 600 alpine and Himalayan plants.

INSHRIACH is on the B970, 4 miles south of Aviemore.

INVERNESS
Inverness

The Highland capital is a place whose history goes back a very long way. There is a record that in 565 St Columba came to visit King Brude of the Picts, and the vitrified fort on the summit of Craig Phadrig — culminating point of a fine forest walk — may have been the hilltop stronghold of the Pictish kings.

Modern Inverness has a pleasant situation, spread along both sides of the sweeping River Ness. There are several footbridges, including a series which link the wooded Ness Islands to pathways on both banks.

Directly above the river, Inverness Castle is an imposing pink-sandstone building erected as the court house in 1834. Its immediate predecessor on the site was blown up by the Jacobites, in a spectacularly mismanaged explosion in 1746. In front of the castle, a statue of Flora MacDonald gazes westward across the river, forest and mountain view.

Other notable buildings in Inverness include the ornate Victorian Gothic town house; St Andrew's Cathedral and, beside it, the modern Eden Court Theatre incorporating the original bishop's residence; the clock tower which is all that remains of the fort built in the 1650s by Cromwell's troops; and the restored, late 16th-century Abertarff House, headquarters of the Gaelic association, *An Comunn Gaidhealach.*

Out of doors, Inverness has good salmon and sea-trout fishing on the Ness. There are two golf courses, extensive parks and sports grounds. And from the Caledonian Canal basin, cruises leave for Loch Ness.

INVERNESS is where the A9 and the A82 meet the A96.

KINGUSSIE
Badenoch and Strathspey

Often called the capital of Badenoch, Kingussie was no more than a few houses round a church until 1799, when the Duke of Gordon advertised leases of ground. In the years which followed, it developed into a neatly laid-out little town of traditional stone-built houses.

The Highland Folk Museum transferred to Kingussie in 1944. Set

Twinkling lights along the River Ness illuminate the castle above

in six acres, it includes indoor and outdoor collections, as well as complete buildings like a Lewis 'black house'.

Kingussie has a testing golf course, designed by Harry Vardon, in the birchwood hills which rise to the north. Above it, and a wide-ranging viewpoint over the Spey Valley to the Cairngorms, is the craggy 1581-ft summit of Creag Bheag.

KINGUSSIE is on the A86, 11 miles south-west of Aviemore.

KINLOCHLEVEN
Lochaber

This industrial village in the dominating mountain landscape at the head of Loch Leven was built in Edwardian times to serve an aluminium factory. The classic *Children of the Dead End* by Patrick MacGill describes the harsh, wild life of the 'navvies' who worked on the dams and tunnels of the factory's hydro-electric scheme.

The West Highland Way comes into Kinlochleven from the south-east, down a steep birchwood glen on the old Devil's Staircase military road from Glencoe. It passes the penstock — where the water from the Blackwater Reservoir is fed into the huge pipes which supply the factory's turbines.

North-west of the village, the Way zig-zags up towards its final mountain crossing to Fort William.

KINLOCHLEVEN is on the B863, 7 miles east of Glencoe village.

LOCH AN EILEIN
Badenoch and Strathspey

In the heart of the superb Rothiemurchus pinewoods, with their scattered larch and pine and undergrowth of juniper, Loch an Eilein is on the edge of the 100 square-mile Cairngorms

In summertime, the cool, clear waters of Loch an Eilein are framed by deep green forests of larch and pine

National Nature Reserve.

A nature trail round the loch passes through the territory of roe deer, red squirrel and wildcat. Birds resident here range from the bulky capercaillie, with its bubbling and cork-popping call, to the tiny goldcrest.

Many species of wild duck feed on the loch. On the island which gives it its name there is a ruined 15th-century castle. Ospreys were last recorded nesting on the castle ruins in 1899; now their place has been taken by jackdaws.

🚗 *LOCH AN EILEIN is off the B970, 2½ miles south of Aviemore.*

LOCH GARTEN
Badenoch and Strathspey

A few years after they left Loch an Eilein, ospreys were lost to Scotland for almost half a century. Then, in 1954, a pair returned to Loch Garten, among the pines of Abernethy Forest. There has been a nest here ever since, in a reserve of the Royal Society for the Protection of Birds.

From the time the ospreys arrive in April until they leave again in August, their nest is in clear view from the visitor centre. And in the lochs of the Spey Valley, the adult birds will sometimes be seen, swooping down on pike or trout.

🚗 *LOCH GARTEN is off the B970, 2 miles east of Boat of Garten.*

MONIACK CASTLE
Inverness

In latitudes and temperatures where grapes cannot be grown outdoors, many private houses and stately homes in the Highlands nevertheless manage to produce their own wine — from elder flowers and rowan berries, and the sap of the silver birch.

Only at white-towered Moniack Castle, a 16th-century Fraser proper-

Nairn boasts some of the most magnificent sandy beaches in Scotland

ty among the fields and woodlands between Inverness and Beauly, is this done on a commercial scale. Highland Wineries were established there in 1979, and are open to the public to demonstrate a wine-making tradition handed down through many generations.

🚗 *MONIACK CASTLE is off the A862, 7 miles west of Inverness.*

NAIRN
Nairn

James VI of Scotland was referring to Nairn when, having also become James I of England, he boasted that in his Scottish kingdom there was a town so long that the people at either end of it could not understand one another's conversation.

Size had nothing to do with it, but for many years Nairn was right on the boundary between Gaelic and English speakers.

The modern town is built on both banks of the River Nairn, with sandy beaches extending east and west. Its one-time fishing harbour is now mainly given over to yachts and dinghies.

The old Fishertown — once a prosperous exporter of salted herring — survives in neat rows of restored cottages, and has its own museum to recall the days when Nairn was one of the most important centres of the Moray Firth fishing.

Nairn is a well-known and championship-standard golfing resort, with links courses backed by gorse and pine. There are footpaths along both banks of the wooded riverside, and a heritage trail round the town's most notable buildings.

🚗 *NAIRN is on the A96, 16 miles north-east of Inverness.*

NEPTUNE'S STAIRCASE
Lochaber

Notorious as probably the most lackadaisical construction job ever tackled in the Highlands, Thomas Telford's flight of eight locks at the southern entrance to the Caledonian Canal was started in 1805 and not completed until six years later. Even then, the contractor's masonry work was so poorly done that — together with other problems elsewhere — it delayed the official opening of the canal until 1822.

Soon christened Neptune's Staircase, these locks nevertheless remain the most impressive piece of canal design in Scotland, above a sea-loch and in full view of Ben Nevis across the water.

🚗 *NEPTUNE'S STAIRCASE is at Banavie on the A830, 3 miles north of Fort William.*

NETHY BRIDGE
Badenoch and Strathspey

Now a quiet holiday village within easy reach of the Cairngorms and the Speyside pinewoods, and with its own golf course nearby, Nethy Bridge shows few signs of the furious industrial activity which overtook it in the 18th century.

On the rocky banks of the River Nethy which cascades through the village is the site of a charcoal-fired iron furnace, in short-lived production from 1729.

Charcoal was made in the local forests, and the iron-ore was carried by pony-trains from a remote mine in the hills 15 miles to the east. Timber was also floated to the Spey, where great rafts of it were navigated down-river to the boat-building yards on the Moray Firth.

🚗 *NETHY BRIDGE is on the B970, 5 miles south of Grantown-on-Spey.*

NEWTONMORE
Badenoch and Strathspey

This is the heart of Macpherson country, and the first clan museum in Scotland was opened here in 1952. The Macphersons' March is a feature of Newtonmore Highland Games, every year on the first weekend in August.

The long, stone-built village began to grow up in the early 19th century,

populated partly by farmers who had been forced out of Glen Banchor to make way for sheep.

Pony-trekking was introduced to the Highlands here. There is angling on the Spey, its tributaries and lochans in the hills. Newtonmore has a beautifully situated riverside golf course. But the biggest cheers here are for shinty: Newtonmore's team has been the most consistently successful in the history of this essentially Highlanders' sport.

🚗 *NEWTONMORE is on the A86, 14 miles south-west of Aviemore.*

ROTHIEMURCHUS
Badenoch and Strathspey

This famous estate, owned since 1580 by the Grants of Rothiemurchus, extends from the east bank of the Spey to the 4248-ft summit of Braeriach on the Cairngorm plateau.

Its facilities include the Moormore picnic area in heathery pinewood beside the tumbling River Luineag, the outflow from Loch Morlich; a rainbow-trout fishery; low-level walks among pine and birchwoods; and hill-walkers' rights-of-way through the pass of the Lairig Ghru towards Deeside, and into the huge corrie of Loch Einich, a glacial valley encircled by prodigious rock buttresses and scree-runs.

There is a visitor centre at Inverdruie, once the headquarters of those characters who built and floated the timber-rafts down the Spey.

🚗 *INVERDRUIE visitor centre is on the B970, 1 mile south-east of Aviemore.*

RUTHVEN BARRACKS
Badenoch and Strathspey

In 1719 the hilltop site of an old castle overlooking an important Spey crossing was chosen as the location of a

new government fort. The Jacobites besieged it in 1745, but got no change out of the formidable Sergeant Molloy, who held them off with a defensive force of only a dozen men.

The Jacobites returned the following year, and this time burned the barracks out. That was no good omen for them, because it was back at Ruthven — which is now a floodlit ancient monument — that Bonnie Prince Charlie, after the defeat at Culloden, formally disbanded the last-ever Jacobite army.

🚗 *RUTHVEN BARRACKS are on the B970, 1 mile south-east of Kingussie.*

STRATHSPEY RAILWAY
Badenoch and Strathspey

Until 1863, Boat of Garten was simply the location of a chain-ferry across the Spey. Then the Inverness and Perth Junction Railway arrived, and a fair-sized village grew up.

The railway closed in 1968. Exactly ten years later, the volunteer-run Strathspey Railway began scheduled summer services on five miles of restored line through pine and birchwood to Aviemore Speyside.

Many of its furnishings arrived here after ending their useful life on main-line routes — the station buildings from Dalnaspidal, the footbridge from Longmorn, the turntable from Kyle of Lochalsh.

The Strathspey Railway has a comprehensive stock of steam and diesel locomotives, carriages and wagons; and there are plans to extend it down-river to Grantown-on-Spey.

🚗 *BOAT OF GARTEN is 6 miles north-east of Aviemore.*

Eerily silhouetted against a darkening sky, the grim ruins of Ruthven Barracks

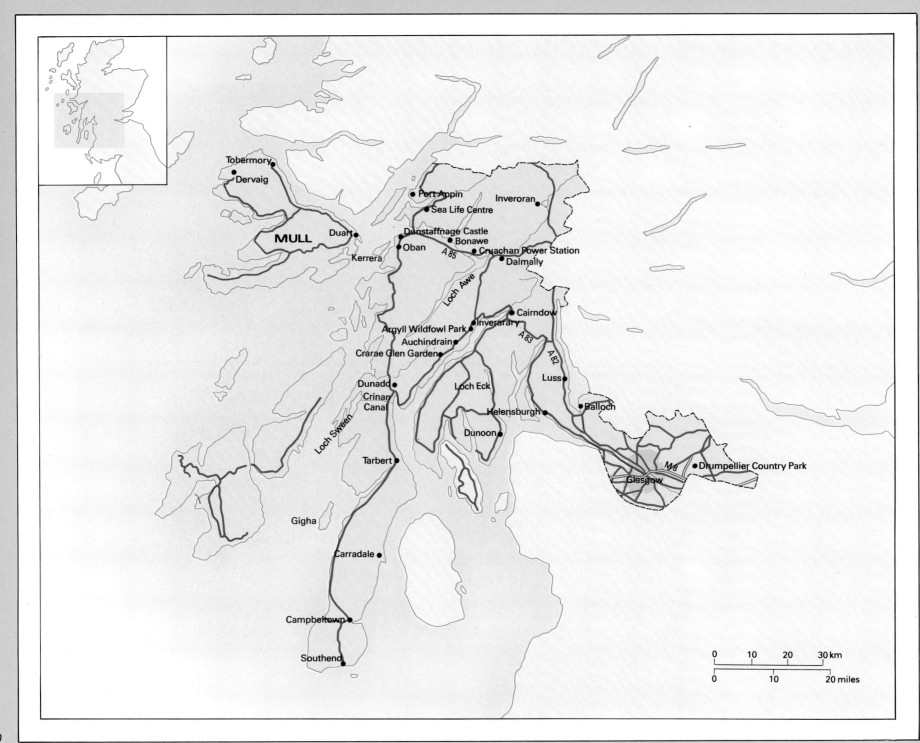

MULL

Tobermory
Dervaig

Port Appin
Sea Life Centre
Inveroran

Duart
Dunstaffnage Castle
Bonawe
Oban
Kerrera
A85
Cruachan Power Station
Dalmally

Loch Awe

Cairndow
Argyll Wildfowl Park
Inverarary
Auchindrain
A83
Crarae Glen Garden
A82

Dunadd
Luss
Crinan
Canal
Loch Eck
Balloch
Helensburgh
Loch Sween
Dunoon
Tarbert
M8
Drumpellier Country Park
Glasgow

Gigha

Carradale

Campbeltown

Southend

0   10   20   30 km

0   10   20 miles

Dunollie Castle, a hill-top ruin above Oban's sweeping Ganavan Sands, was the home of the Mac Dougall chiefs until the mid 18th century

WHEN SCOTTISH LOCAL government boundaries were re-drawn in 1975, Strathclyde became the country's most important Region — a vast area containing half of Scotland's population, and spreading from the Lowther Hills of the Southern Uplands to some of the Inner Hebrides.

The northern part of Strathclyde therefore stretches from the city of Glasgow to the Atlantic coast and beyond. It includes industrial areas, the museums and galleries for which Glasgow has become world-famous, part of Loch Lomond, great tracts of mountain and forest and lochside in Cowal, and a scattering of islands off the west coast — Islay and Jura, Colonsay, Coll and Tiree, Iona and Mull.

There are forest walks, nature trails and compact, rock-climbers' mountain ranges like the 'Arrochar Alps' between Loch Lomond and Loch Fyne. And the 'great gardens of Argyll' justify the name.

Famous castles are to be seen here, like the ones whose fire-beacons used to flash messages of war and peace along the Sound of Mull, and the ancestral homes still lived in by the Campbells and the Macleans.

But there are many relics of the hazy centuries well before the upsurge of the clans. This is also the country of Dalriada, the first settlement made by the Scots when they arrived from Ireland. They crowned their kings on a hilltop fortress overlooking a fertile valley whose cairns and standing stones played a significant part in ancient societies.

ARGYLL WILDFOWL PARK
Argyll and Bute

Established in 1984, in 55 acres of forest, open ground and pebble beach on the shore of Loch Fyne, this unusual nature park has expanded far beyond the limit suggested by its title. In scattered ponds it has a collection of well-known wildfowl species, as well as rarer breeds like Fulvous Tree Ducks and Lesser Magellan Geese.

But the plantation is now home to roe deer, wildcats and even wallabies; and one section is entirely given over to owls. The total number of bird and animal species in the park is now well over 100. With its forest, shore and nearby grazing land, it also attracts passing birds which temporarily 'join' the collection.

ARGYLL WILDFOWL PARK is on the A83, 1½ miles south-west of Inveraray.

AUCHINDRAIN
Argyll and Bute

This partly open-air museum is unique. Auchindrain was the last farming settlement in the whole of Scotland to persevere with the old multiple-tenancy system — its 4000 acres, mostly hill grazing for sheep and cattle, were farmed as a unit, not by a single family, but by several families living in the same group of cottages. That arrangement came to an end only in 1935, long after it had been given up elsewhere.

Some of the 18th- and 19th-century cottages are furnished from different periods in Auchindrain's history. And the six arable fields which remain at the 30-acre heart of the old farm, protected from the advancing ranks of conifers, are steadily being reclaimed.

AUCHINDRAIN is on the A83, 5 miles south-west of Inveraray.

BALLOCH
Dumbarton

Built on both banks of the River Leven, where it leaves Loch Lomond, Balloch is the start of many of the cruises on the loch, and there are boatyards and dozens of moorings. A wildlife park occupies part of the Cameron estate on the west bank, while Balloch Castle Country Park rising from the east bank is the headquarters of a countryside ranger service.

It is the land around an early 19th-century hilltop castle, set above sweeping lawns. The park has a tree trail with several rarities, a keep-fit trail, informal woodland walks and a quiet walled garden.

A much older castle survives only as a grassy mound near the loch. It was the seat of the Earls of Lennox, who transferred around 1390 to a more secure location on the offshore island of Inchmurrin.

BALLOCH is off the A82, 3 miles north of Dumbarton.

BONAWE
Argyll and Bute

The most famous, and by far the best-restored, of Scotland's 18th-century charcoal ironworks is in a truly incongruous setting, looking out to the mountains flanking a lovely sea-loch.

Auchindrain's old whitewashed farming cottages are now part of a unique museum complex

English industrialists founded the Lorn Furnace above Loch Etive in 1753, shipping in the ore from Furness in Lancashire. They built a self-contained village around the works, which were out-dated almost before they went into production, because charcoal-fired furnaces which needed close-by woodlands were being replaced by coke-fired operations nearer the coalfields.

Bonawe produced cannonballs and shot as well as pig-iron during more than 120 years of operation. Unused for over a century, its buildings now house a fascinating exhibition of the industry's techniques and favoured locations.

BONAWE is immediately north of Taynuilt on the A85.

CAIRNDOW
Argyll and Bute

An old coaching village long since bypassed by the modern main road, Cairndow shelters below steep, sheep-grazed hills near the head of Loch Fyne. On a fine day, green hills, blue sky and white cottages reflect pleasantly in the loch.

John Keats, the poet, stayed at the village inn during an energetic walking tour when he came over the stiff climb of the Rest and be Thankful from Loch Long.

The white-walled octagonal church has a square tower and some curious headstones in the graveyard that surrounds it.

Nearby is Strone woodland garden, laid out along both banks of the Kinglass Water. There are masses of springtime daffodils, a fine collection of rhododendrons and azaleas, and, at 200 ft, one of the trees in the spectacular pinetum is the tallest in Britain.

CAIRNDOW is off the A83, 12 miles north-west of Arrochar.

The island of Davaar lies in the mouth of Campbeltown Loch

CAMPBELTOWN
Argyll and Bute

Originally on the territory of the MacDonalds, this town at the head of an east-facing sea-loch took its modern name in 1667, after it had come into the hands of their rivals, the Campbell Earls of Argyll.

Campbeltown was a great fishing and whisky-distilling centre, as the local museum shows; but the 32 distilleries that were once on record have dwindled to two.

In the mouth of Campbeltown Loch is the hilly, lighthouse island of Davaar, reached at low water by a walk along the edge of a shingle bank. In 1887 a local man called Archibald MacKinnon painted a dream-inspired Crucifixion scene on an inner wall. He went back to renew the colours 47 years later, and the painting is still kept freshened up.

There is a fine golf course on the links of Machrihanish, due west of Campbeltown, behind the dunes of a three-and-a-half mile Atlantic beach.

CAMPBELTOWN is on the A83, 52 miles south of Tarbert.

CARRADALE
Argyll and Bute

A link with the faraway Viking past, Carradale is a fishing and holiday village on the coast of Kintyre, with almost mile-long sands at the head of a south-facing bay, and a river winding down a narrow farmland valley between forested hills.

There is a golf course, sailing and windsurfing in the main bay, and many smaller bays down unobtrusive side-roads. Salmon and trout-anglers fish the river, and forest walks lead to viewpoints over Kilbrannan Sound to the mountains of Arran.

Roe and fallow deer browse in the plantations, there is a herd of wild

33

Cabin cruisers follow the route taken by Queen Victoria's royal barge in 1847 on the Crinan Canal

goats on Carradale Point, and this is the hunting ground of kestrel, buzzard, hen harrier and golden eagle.

🚗 *CARRADALE is on the B879, 23 miles south of Tarbert.*

CRARAE GLEN GARDEN
Argyll and Bute

First planted around 1912 on both sides of a handsome glen, down which a burn tumbles on its way to Loch Fyne, this is a garden where tall sheltering trees protect a glorious variety of flowering shrubs. Many were brought from the Himalayas in the garden's earliest years.

Run by a charitable trust, Crarae has a brilliant display of rhododendrons in spring and early summer. But its magnolias and other later-flowering shrubs keep the garden bright and lively right through until the autumn. Much of the tree cover has been thinned so as to re-open the splendid views over the loch.

🚗 *CRARAE GLEN GARDEN is on the A83, 11 miles south-west of Inveraray.*

CRINAN CANAL
Argyll and Bute

Although work started in 1794 on the nine-mile waterway from Ardrishaig to Crinan, it was 23 years later that the Crinan Canal was satisfactorily completed.

After Queen Victoria's voyage to Crinan in 1847, when her lavishly furnished barge was drawn along by three horses, the canal was publicised as part of the 'Royal Route'.

It has 15 locks and seven swing bridges — two of which, Miller's Bridge and Bellanoch, are in particularly fine settings. The towpath,

Dervaig Church has an unusual, Irish-style pencil tower

in stretches doubling as a public road, makes an excellent walk, especially towards the west end, where it passes the wooded cliffs around Crinan, with magnificent views over a sea-loch to the Poltalloch hills.

Crinan itself is an attractive but bewilderingly scattered village with a busy canal basin. At Crinan Harbour — separate from the canal — a network of forest walks leads to high-level viewpoints over the Sound of Jura.

ARDRISHAIG is on the A83, 1½ miles south of Lochgilphead; Crinan is on the B841, 7 miles west of Lochgilphead.

CRUACHAN POWER STATION
Argyll and Bute

Ben Cruachan is Scotland's 'hollow mountain'. Deep within it, in an excavated chamber big enough to accommodate a seven-storey block of flats, is the machine hall of a pumped-storage hydro-electric generating scheme opened in 1965.

Water is piped from a reservoir in a corrie high on the mountain slopes. During the day, that water turns the generating turbines. At off-peak periods, the turbines are reversed so that water from Loch Awe is pumped back up to the reservoir.

There is a very informative visitor centre on the lochside, from which minibus tours are arranged along the road-tunnel right into the heart of the mountain.

CRUACHAN power station is on the A85, 6 miles west of Dalmally.

DALMALLY
Argyll and Bute

Although it grew up around a mid-Victorian railway station, this is a village in several separated parts. It is surrounded by hills and glens, and is bounded to the north by the lower reaches of the River Orchy, a good angling water whose pebbly banks are popular for picnics.

Dalmally has a busy livestock market and a shinty field. Its parish church is on a rise of ground where two channels of the Orchy have created an often unnoticed island.

A narrow road climbs from the station to Monument Hill — named after the impressive memorial to one of Gaeldom's most famous poets, Duncan Ban MacIntyre — and opens up a majestic view to Ben Cruachan and the tangle of islands in Loch Awe.

DALMALLY is on the A85, 11 miles west of Tyndrum.

DERVAIG
Argyll and Bute

At the very end of the 18th century, 26 matching houses were built near the head of Loch Cuin in the north-west of Mull, and they still form the major part of the village of Dervaig.

Overlooking the tidal mouth of the River Bellart, which flows into the sea-loch, Kilmore parish church is highly unusual. The original church of 1755 was dismantled early this century, and the architect of its replacement included a round, pencil-tower belfry in a style he had often seen in Ireland.

Anglers fish the Bellart for salmon and sea-trout. Dervaig also attracts many visitors to its Old Byre Heritage Centre, where the history of the area is documented and explained.

At the enterprising Mull Little Theatre, whose audiences are limited to intimate gatherings of around 40 people, visitors can enjoy a variety of live entertainment throughout the year.

DERVAIG is on the B8073, 6 miles south-west of Tobermory.

DRUMPELLIER COUNTRY PARK
Monklands

Referred to in charters from as early as the 12th century, Drumpellier was handed over in 1919 to Coatbridge town council. It includes woodlands of beech and oak, ash and sycamore and rhododendron thickets; lawns and a pair of lochs; two nature trails and pathways along the banks of the old Monkland Canal.

There is a very good visitor centre on the north shore of Lochend Loch, which is stocked with trout and is also the nesting-place of mallards, coots and moorhens. The most notable birds here, though, are the mute and whooper swans.
➤ *DRUMPELLIER COUNTRY PARK visitor centre is 2 miles northwest of Coatbridge town centre.*

DUART
Argyll and Bute

The two castles which face each other across Duart Bay on Mull could hardly be more different; but both are still owned and occupied by the families which had them built, and both are open to the public.

Duart Castle itself, a 14th-century fortress dominating the entrance to the Sound of Mull, is the home of the 27th chief of the Macleans of Duart and Morvern. The Macleans were a powerful clan, and displays in the castle show how they figured in many important Highland and island affairs.

Torosay is the work of two notable Victorian architects. David Bryce designed the castle in the 1850s with familiar 'baronial' flourishes, and Sir Robert Lorimer laid out the gardens with their balustraded lawns and Italian-style statue walk.

Between Torosay and the ferry-

Pipe bands create a colourful spectacle in the streets of Dunoon

terminal village of Craignure there is a narrow-gauge railway whose leisurely schedule allows plenty of time for photography.
➤ *TOROSAY CASTLE is off the A849, 1 mile south of Craignure; Duart Castle is on a side-road which leaves the A849 south of Torosay.*

DUNADD
Argyll and Bute

The grass-topped rock outcrop of Dunadd, with its naturally fortified summit, stands above the reclaimed farmlands of Crinan Moss, once a marshy inlet of the sea. Carvings near the summit are traditionally connected with the crowning of the monarchs of the Celtic kingdom of Dalriada, founded at the beginning of the 6th century AD.

Dalriada grew in strength and territory until, in 843, it absorbed the kingdom of the Picts; and that marked the beginning of a country recognisably like modern Scotland.

Although the capital then moved elsewhere, Dunadd remains a notably atmospheric site. And it looks over the Kilmartin valley, whose standing stones, cairns and mysterious carvings go back to the time of Dunadd's own earliest history as a Dark Age hill-fort in the second millenium BC.
➤ *DUNADD is off the A816, 4 miles north of Lochgilphead.*

DUNOON
Argyll and Bute

In the early 19th century, as steamships began to operate on the Firth of Clyde, Dunoon and its satellite village of Kirn grew up as favourite places for Glasgow people to have weekend and holiday homes.

Dunoon is still a significant holiday resort, with a long promenade of sea-facing villas and hotels linking it with Kirn. Every year it plays host to the Cowal Highland Games, where no fewer than 150 pipe bands can be seen marching in line ahead and the whole town celebrates.

Above the pier, in the hillside park which occupies the site of the old Dunoon Castle, is a statue to a local girl called Mary Campbell — Robert Burns's 'Highland Mary'. They were about to marry and emigrate to the West Indies, but Mary suddenly took ill and died. Burns decided, after all, to stay with his own folk in Scotland.
➤ *DUNOON is on the A815, across the Firth of Clyde from the east-side car-ferry terminal at Gourock.*

Scottish forests

Britain's first forest park was established in Argyll in 1935, but extensive woods of birch and pine were growing here thousands of years before that — the birch an excellent self-propagator, the pine eventually the first conifer to be cultivated in plantations.

Millions of acres of the old Caledonian Forest were sacrificed to farming — whether by the clearing of land for the plough, or by the grazing of sheep, or by the practice of burning the moorland to encourage new grass to grow.

Foresters tend to be sceptical that other popular explanations for the disappearance of the original woodlands — deliberate

Forestry plantations at Dalchork

destruction of the hiding-places of wolves and human bandits, or colossal storms, or natural fires — can have had much large-scale, long-term effect.

Now there are modern commercial plantations — mostly of spruce and larch, Scots and Lodgepole pine — in many parts of north Strathclyde, but especially on the hills and lochsides of Argyll; even on the rugged island of Jura. They provide nature trails and picnic places, bridle paths, viewpoints and holiday villages.

But areas of older forests survive, and there are some real showpieces. Above Kilmun on the Holy Loch, for instance, the Commission maintains an arboretum, with steep and winding pathways through plots of forest and ornamental trees, and many flowering shrubs.

And at Glen Nant, a Forest Nature Reserve encloses an old woodland harvested on the coppice system for almost 120 years, to provide charcoal for the ironworks at Bonawe on Loch Etive, themselves a splendidly restored and informative ancient monument.

Woodland for all to enjoy at Galloway Forest Park

DUNSTAFFNAGE CASTLE
Argyll and Bute

More than 20 generations of Campbells have been hereditary Captains of Dunstaffnage, but this strategically-placed castle guarding the entrance to Loch Etive was begun in the 13th century by their predecessors, the MacDougall Lords of Lorn.

Dunstaffnage was garrisoned, attacked and defended in many wars, from the time of the Jacobites — Flora MacDonald was briefly held prisoner here after it was discovered how she had helped Bonnie Prince Charlie, but she was gently treated.

Since 1958 the curtain-walled castle, which from the open sea stands on the summit of a rocky outcrop, but on the other side has lawns rising from a sheltered bay, has been looked after as an ancient monument.

DUNSTAFFNAGE CASTLE is signposted from Dunbeg, on the A85, 2 miles north-east of Oban.

GIGHA
Argyll and Bute

In the days of the Norsemen, Gigha was named Gudey — 'the Good Island'. It is the most southerly of the Inner Hebrides, famous for the sheltered sub-tropical gardens of Achamore House.

Established in 1945, the gardens feature a dazzling display of rhododendrons, as well as trees and other flowering shrubs from South America and Australasia. In 1962 the plant collection was presented to the National Trust for Scotland; but the grounds — although open to visitors — remain in private hands.

Otherwise, Gigha is a fertile dairy-farming island, with a single village at Ardminish, fine sandy beaches backed by springy machair turf, fishing lochs, yacht anchorages and many ancient standing stones.

🚗 *GIGHA is reached by car-ferry from Tayinloan, on the A83, 19 miles south of Tarbert.*

GLASGOW
City of Glasgow

Although it was one of the power-houses of the Industrial Revolution, Glasgow has developed into a city with more than 70 public parks and some of the finest art galleries in Britain.

In the whole of Scotland, the place which attracts more visitors than any other — a million of them in a year — is the Burrell Gallery set in the 361 acres of woodlands, lawns, nature trails and grazing land of Pollok Park.

The magnificent 8000-piece collection of paintings, tapestries, ceramics, stonework, stained glass and silverware was presented to the city by the ship-owning millionaire Sir William Burrell.

But 'the Burrell' is not the only important building in the park. The 18th-century Palladian mansion of Pollok House is a museum showing off elegant plasterwork, furniture and furnishings, and one of Britain's finest collections of Spanish art.

Other major collections are housed in the Art Gallery and Museum in Kelvingrove Park, and in the People's Palace — which concentrates on the city's own social and industrial history — on Glasgow Green.

A monument nearby celebrates the spot where, in the course of a Sunday-morning stroll in the year 1765, James Watt — mulling over his ideas about steam engines — was struck by the notion of the fundamental improvement which transformed them into reliable and economical power-sources, and made the In-

dustrial Revolution a possibility.

Much of Glasgow is Victorian, like the Italian Renaissance-style City Chambers, where guided tours show off beautiful ceilings, mosaic floors and the superb staircase with its alabaster pillars, Numidian and Carrara marble.

Glasgow was also the native city of the architect Charles Rennie Mackintosh, many of whose buildings — like the School of Art — attract worldwide attention. His own house, with its original scheme of furnishings, has been reconstructed in the tower of Glasgow University's Hunterian Art Gallery.

Away from art and architecture, Glasgow is also the home of Scottish Opera, Scottish Ballet and two full-scale symphony orchestras.

🚗 *GLASGOW is 45 miles west of Edinburgh.*

Glasgow Cathedral is pre-Reformation Gothic

The Venetian-style Templeton factory on Glasgow Green

Hill House, Helensburgh, is a delight, both outside and in, for lovers of Rennie Mackintosh's *art nouveau* style

HELENSBURGH
Dumbarton

One of several towns on the Firth of Clyde which expanded after the railway arrived from Glasgow, Helensburgh was founded some years earlier — in 1776 — by Sir James Colquhoun, who named it after his wife.

On the promenade there is a monument to Henry Bell, whose *Comet* of 1812 was the world's first sea-going steamship. His wife kept the family financially afloat by running a fine hotel.

Helensburgh was the birthplace of television pioneer John Logie Baird. One of his original 'televisors' is preserved in the local library.

But the showpiece of the town is the Edwardian villa called Hill House, designed by Charles Rennie Mackintosh. Now owned by the National Trust for Scotland, it retains the furniture and furnishings of Mackintosh's *art nouveau* style.

🚗 *HELENSBURGH is on the A814, 8 miles north-west of Dumbarton.*

INVERARAY
Argyll and Bute

The northern aspect of this elegant little town is a line of whitewashed Georgian buildings and archways facing Loch Fyne.

Originally, the town stood near Inveraray Castle, home of the Dukes of Argyll who head the senior branch of Clan Campbell.

But in 1743, when the 3rd Duke decided to have a much grander castle built, the old town was cleared away and the present one was created, virtually all of a piece.

The castle has an extensive collection of portraits and tapestries on show; and its armoury hall displays something like 1300 broadswords, muskets and pikes.

Memories of a later style of war are revived in a nearby museum. In the 1940s, Inveraray was the training centre for the Combined Operations unit which planned and rehearsed the assault landing techniques put into practice on the coasts of Norway, Italy, North Africa and Normandy.

In the town itself, the Bell Tower is not only an excellent viewpoint over the loch; it also has a ten-bell peal regarded as the finest in Scotland, installed as the Campbell war memorial.

🚗 *INVERARAY is on the A83, 22 miles west of Arrochar.*

INVERORAN
Argyll and Bute

Now little more than a lonely hotel patronised by walkers, mountaineers and anglers, this was once an overnight stance for man and beast on the busy cattle-drovers' route from Fort William; and the military road to the fort there was built through Inveroran in the 1750s.

The West Highland Way approaches it from the south-east over the winding viewpoint pass of the Mam Carraigh, and continues north by a remote, exposed route to Glencoe with tremendous views west to the outstanding peaks and corries of the Black Mount range, and east over the almost trackless lochside peat mosses of Rannoch Moor.

🚗 *INVERORAN is on the A8005, 3 miles north-west of Bridge of Orchy.*

KERRERA
Argyll and Bute

The long island of Kerrera which shelters the harbour and anchorages of Oban Bay is much more than simply a windbreak; it is also an exhilarating place for walkers.

On the coast of the narrow Sound of Kerrera is the area still called the King's Field, where Alexander II died in 1249 during an expedition round the West Highland castles.

The ruins of the 16th-century MacDougall stronghold of Gylen stand on a rocky peninsula on the south coast. Nearby, an old drove road — once part of the complicated route by which cattle from Mull were driven to the mainland markets — leads back across the heart of the island to the ferry.

⛴ *THE KERRERA ferry is reached by taking the Gallanach road from the centre of Oban.*

39

Shades of autumn in the Younger Botanic Garden, south of Loch Eck

conifer plantations, rocky cliffs and lateral glens of open grazing land, this narrow and gently winding loch is one of the most striking inland waters in Scotland.

Sailing, canoeing and angling are all encouraged. The main road along the east shore has water's-edge parking and picnic places. A walking route follows the west shore, and there are — as in the rest of the Argyll Forest Park — others to viewpoints all over the forested hills.

Just south of the loch, the superb Younger Botanic Garden features a Wellingtonia avenue planted in the 1860s, more than 250 species of rhododendron and one of the best collections of Asiatic conifers in the country.

LOCH ECK is on the A815, north of Dunoon.

LOCH SWEEN
Argyll and Bute

This sea-loch penetrating deep into the hills of Knapdale, where it begins among the labyrinth of forested inlets, takes its name from what is probably the oldest stone-built castle on the Scottish mainland. Castle Sween was begun in the 12th century, but has been in ruins since its final besieging in 1647.

There are three villages round the loch. Tayvallich is an attractive sailing centre with a more than semicircular bay. Achnamara is a forestry settlement on one of the long upper inlets. And Kilmory Knap, looking out towards the island peaks of Jura, has the roofed-over ruin of a 12th-century chapel with a notable collection of carved and decorated gravestones dating back over 1000 years.

LOCH SWEEN is south of Crinan, reached by the B8025 from Bellanoch.

LOCH AWE
Argyll and Bute

From the scree-slopes of the Pass of Brander to the village of Ford, the 27 miles of Loch Awe are surrounded by very fine mountain and forest scenery.

Inverliever Forest, on the western side, has miles of walks, picnic places and viewpoints. A famous name by the water's edge there is New York — a long-since abandoned 18th-century hamlet.

Well-known fishing hotels at Taychreggan and Portsonachan face each other across the narrowest stretch of the loch. They were originally built as inns at either side of the main ferry crossing.

Several notable buildings have Campbell connections. The ruined island stronghold of Innischonnel Castle was where the ancestors of the Duke of Argyll established themselves in the 12th century, long before making the move to Inveraray.

Kilchurn Castle, a dramatically situated ancient monument on a marshy peninsula towered over by Ben Cruachan, was built in the 15th century by the Campbells of Glenorchy, later Earls of Breadalbane, before they too moved elsewhere.

On a smaller scale, St Conan's Kirk on the outskirts of Lochawe village, built between 1881 and 1930, was designed by Walter Campbell of Innischonain to have an almost eccentric variety of architectural styles and details.

THE A85 reaches the north shore of Loch Awe 1 mile west of Dalmally.

LOCH ECK
Argyll and Bute

The steep hillsides around Loch Eck are mostly owned by the Forestry Commission; but in its mixture of

McCaig's Tower, set high on a hill above Oban, is perhaps the town's best-known feature

LUSS
Dumbarton

Although the Colquhouns have been lairds of Luss on Loch Lomondside for nearly 800 years, the present village of attractive single-storey cottages dates only from the middle of the 19th century.

Luss has a shingle beach, a pier for the Loch Lomond cruises and a splendid view northwards to the 3192-ft Ben Lomond. Its dignified parish church was built in 1875 in memory of one of the lairds, who was drowned in a winter storm.

A narrow road climbs into Glen Luss, opening up a panoramic view of the wooded islands which crowd the southern end of the loch.

LUSS is on the A82, 8 miles north of Balloch.

OBAN
Argyll and Bute

Holiday resort, railhead, yacht anchorage, fishing harbour, ferry terminal for half a dozen islands — Oban is a place of constant comings and goings. Its Victorian houses climb from the shore of a bay, and it is a town with many walks on ridges and wooded hills.

McCaig's Tower is the classic high-level viewpoint — a massive, turn-of-the-century round tower in Argyll granite with arched window openings. In daytime, it provides breathtaking views over Kerrera to the mountains of Mull and Morvern; later, the attraction is the other way round, as the tower is floodlit against the evening sky.

Another favoured view is from Pulpit Hill, the wooded crag which rises south of the bay.

Northwards, the shore road to Ganavan Sands passes below the hilltop ruin of Dunollie Castle, the home until the mid-18th century of the MacDougall chiefs, whose modern home is nearby.

🚗 *OBAN is at the junction of the A85 from Dalmally and the A816 from Lochgilphead.*

PORT APPIN
Argyll and Bute

Although steamer calls are a thing of the past, Port Appin still has a passenger ferry to the north end of the island of Lismore.

From the wooded ridge above the cottages which lead to the jetty, there is a wide-ranging view over Lismore and the skerries north of it to the rugged hills of Kingairloch. A very fine coastal walk circles the ridge.

North of the village is the restored and spectacularly located island tower of Castle Stalker, once a royal hunting resort and a stronghold of the Stewarts.

🚗 *PORT APPIN is reached by a side-road off the A828, 22 miles north of Oban*

SEA LIFE CENTRE
Argyll and Bute

Outdoor activities around the village of Barcaldine include forest walks, trout fishing in a hill reservoir, sailing and sea-angling in Loch Creran. The loch is also the base of a commercial fish-farm, whose owners in 1979 established the Sea Life Centre in a pinewood beside a rocky bay.

It has indoor display tanks of fish as different in character and appearance as rays and eels. Herring show off their compulsion to swim in shoals. And twice a day there is a flurry of elegant activity as the seals cavort around while waiting to be fed in their outdoor pool.

🚗 *THE SEA LIFE CENTRE is on the A828, 10 miles north of Oban.*

SOUTHEND
Argyll and Bute

This is the last village in Kintyre, with excellent beaches and a fine golf course. On the rock of Dunaverty is the site of a castle taken by the Covenanting army in 1647, when everyone in it was slaughtered.

In a far gentler context, the traditional first landing place in Scotland of the crusading St Columba, when he came over as a missionary from Ireland in 563, was below the cliffs at Keil Point.

Away to the west, a convoluted hill road climbs to the pass known simply as 'The Gap', then plunges down towards the Mull of Kintyre lighthouse, with an impressive over-the-sea view to Rathlin Island and the Antrim coast.

🚗 *SOUTHEND is on the B842, 9 miles south of Campbeltown.*

TARBERT
Argyll and Bute

As it does elsewhere, this name describes a narrow isthmus over which a boat can be manhandled. At the end of the 11th century, tradition insists that Magnus Barefoot craftily ordered his men to haul his galley across the neck of land which connects the peninsula of Kintyre to the rest of the Scottish mainland, and

was thus able to claim Kintyre as Norse territory, within the terms of a treaty which gave the Vikings all the land they could sail a boat round.

After they were driven out of Scotland in 1263, Tarbert continued to be a significant place. Robert the Bruce extended an existing castle here in the 1320s, and the castle ruin still overlooks the sheltered bay.

It was this deep-set bay which caused the present village to be built around it. Tarbert was an ideal harbour for the 19th-century herring fishing in Loch Fyne.

There is less fishing now than there used to be, but Tarbert remains very popular with yachtsmen.

🚗 *TARBERT is on the A83, 14 miles south of Lochgilphead.*

TOBERMORY
Argyll and Bute

This waterside town, where colour-washed houses backed by wooded hills face a natural harbour, never reached the heights of prosperity its creators expected. Tobermory was established at the end of the 1780s by the British Fisheries Society; but once the railways reached the mainland fishing ports, the east coast of Mull was inconveniently far from the markets.

It remains the only town, rather than village, on the whole of Mull, with products ranging from pottery to malt whisky, and it is a famous yachting harbour — the finishing point of a summer race from the Clyde which regularly attracts more than 200 crews.

There are invigorating coastal walks on each side of the bay, the one to the south-east heading into the Forestry Commission's Aros Park. Speculation continues about a Spanish Armada galleon known to have sunk in the bay; but recent research has proved that the treasure-ship it was once believed to be actually reached home safely.

🚗 *TOBERMORY is on the A848, 21 miles north-west of the ferry terminal at Craignure.*

Southend (left) is a popular holiday destination
The colour-washed houses of Tobermory (right)

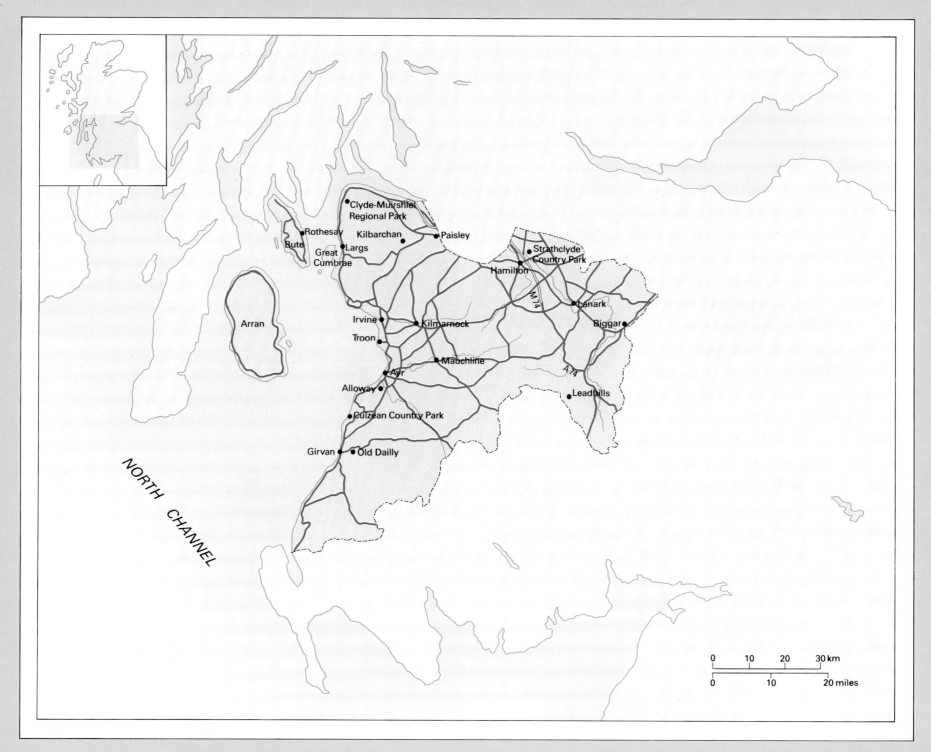

NORTH CHANNEL

Clyde-Muirshiel Regional Park
Rothesay
Bute
Kilbarchan
Paisley
Great Cumbrae
Largs
Strathclyde Country Park
Hamilton
M 74
Lanark
Arran
Irvine
Kilmarnock
Biggar
Troon
Mauchline
A 74
Ayr
Alloway
Leadhills
Culzean Country Park
Girvan
Old Dailly

0   10   20   30 km
0   10   20 miles

South Strathclyde

The streets of Lanark come alive once a year at the time of the Lanimer Week celebrations. Pipe bands create a blaze of colour in this thoroughly Scottish spectacle

LANDSCAPES IN SOUTH STRATHCLYDE are at extremes. There are towns in the industrial belt and — not far away — high, heathery grouse moors. Through the heart of Ayrshire, rich farmland sweeps south to meet up with the forested hills of Carrick. And the gentle, dairy-herd country on some of the islands in the Firth of Clyde contrasts with the massive rock of Ailsa Craig and the granite peaks of Arran.

For generations, the Ayrshire coast and the islands have been places where people go to relax. And this process shows no signs of slackening off. The golf courses on the coastal links regularly play host to the Open Championship. Watersports of all kinds are enjoyed here, on a coast which has marinas, island cruising grounds and sailing schools.

Arran is a splendid centre for hill-walking and rock-climbing. Major recreational areas run from privately-owned woodland estates to a 30,000-acre Regional Park.

This is a country of long memories. Robert Burns's appeal to Scots world-wide has never faded. The Covenanters — stern defenders of the Presbyterian faith in the religious civil wars of the 17th century — are remembered in towns and villages, churches, memorials and the lonely places where, with guards posted against the arrival of government troops whose mission was to hunt them down, they held their services out of doors.

ALLOWAY
Kyle and Carrick

Robert Burns was born here, in what is now a leafy suburb of the town of Ayr, in the house his father built — a thatched-roofed, whitewashed cottage on the edge of his market garden.

Sold off for a time as an inn, the house was later rescued; it and the museum built alongside it are open to the public, showing some of Burns's belongings, paintings and original manuscripts.

The ruined 16th-century Alloway Kirk is much as it was when Burns described how Tam o'Shanter stumbled on the witches and warlocks revelling there.

The furious chase which followed came to its climax at the old single-arch bridge over the River Doon, still preserved. Overlooking the bridge are the gardens of the Burns Monument completed in 1823.

Nearby, the Land o'Burns Centre is an ambitious exhibition of his life and works, and of the Burns Country named after him, with an audio-visual theatre, other displays and an extensive bookshop.

ALLOWAY is on the B7024, south of Ayr.

ARRAN
Cunninghame

With its jagged-outline granite mountains, Arran is like an only-just miniature Skye deposited by accident in the Firth of Clyde. The north-eastern quarter of the island is made up of a series of spectacular peaks and ridges, corries and glens which provide excellent rock-climbing, scrambling and hill-walking as well as the backdrop to some dramatic views.

This is uncompromising mountain country at a substantial height. Goat Fell is the highest point at 2866 ft, and although there is a 'tourist path' to the summit, a jigsaw-puzzle of curving saddles opens up an area best left to experienced ridge-walkers.

But there is a much milder Arran too. Brodick, at the foot of Goat Fell, is the main ferry port on Arran, and its principal holiday resort, with sandy beaches which families have enjoyed for generations.

To the north of the village is the Isle of Arran Heritage Museum, created from a collection of 18th-century croft buildings. A fine golf course — one of seven on the island — is laid out around the tidal lagoons of the Glenrosa Water.

Other sports for which Arran provides facilities include bowls and tennis; riding and pony-trekking; sailing, windsurfing and diving; sea-angling as well as salmon and trout-fishing on the rivers — the Machrie, the Rosa, the Sannox, the Cloy and the oddly-named Sliddery.

Away from the north-eastern mountains, Arran has footpaths through forest plantations and around the southern moorlands where standing stones, cairns and vitrified forts point to a pre-history reaching back to Neolithic times.

Round its 56-mile coast road there are a dozen holiday villages from Lochranza at the north-west corner where whitewashed houses and a ruined castle look over a sea-loch, and a summer car-ferry runs to Claonaig in Kintyre, to Kildonan in the south-east with its view to the rocky lighthouse island of Pladda and — farther away — to the massive 'granite haystack' of Ailsa Craig.

Whiting Bay is a modern village with a walk to a 200-ft waterfall in Glenashdale, and, at Kingscross, the

In the heart of Burns's country are these beautifully-kept gardens and the bridge at Alloway

place from which Robert the Bruce set sail in 1307 to start his guerilla war to wrest back control of Scotland from the English.

Lamlash is the administrative centre of the island, looking out over a sheltered anchorage where the Viking fleet gathered before being defeated, across the Firth, at the Battle of Largs in 1263.

Some of the Vikings with time on their hands carved messages still to be seen on the walls of caves on the 1030-ft Holy Island which holds off the easterly wind. The island can be visited from Lamlash.

The showpiece of Arran is Brodick Castle, whose earliest part dates from the 14th century, although it was completed in its present-day form in the 1840s.

For generations one of the homes of the Dukes of Hamilton, the castle — with its woodlands and the gardens with their extensive collection of flowering shrubs from China, Burma, Tibet, South America, Australia and New Zealand — is now owned by the National Trust for Scotland.

ARDROSSAN on the Ayrshire coast is the departure point for the main Arran car-ferry.

AYR
Kyle and Carrick

Recognised as a royal burgh in the early 13th century, Ayr is a town with two distinct aspects.

One is to the sea. More than two miles of esplanades and fine sandy beaches stretch southwards from the mouth of the River Ayr, passing the headquarters of two sailing clubs. North of the river is the harbour area.

But Ayr is also a county town, the focus of the administrative, trading, business, sporting and social life of central Ayrshire's inland villages,
farms and landed estates.

Either by purchase or by gift, Ayr has gathered into public ownership a remarkable number of parks, gardens, sports grounds and other open spaces.

There are three 18-hole golf courses actually inside the town, as well as major parks at Belleisle, Craigie and Rozelle. The last of these has nature trails, a handsome Georgian mansion used for exhibitions, an art gallery and a sculpture garden. The Dam Park is the venue, every August, for Scotland's largest flower show.

The old racecourse is now given over to sports fields, while the present-day racecourse, home of the Ayr Gold Cup and the Scottish Grand National, is the busiest and most important centre of Flat and National Hunt racing in the country.

Robert Burns was baptised in the Auld Kirk of Ayr, and the town, naturally, keeps his memory alive. Burns Statue Square should be one of the architectural features of the place, but some of the modern buildings sadly let it down.

In the High Street, the Tam o'Shanter Museum is given over to Burns displays. In Burns's day the building was a brewery, and one of the farmers who supplied it with malted grain was none other than Douglas Graham of Shanter — the original of the ballad's hero Tam.

AYR is 32 miles south-west of Glasgow.

BIGGAR
Clydesdale

In 1451, James II granted Biggar its burgh charter, and the right to hold weekly markets. Over the years, it developed into a pleasant, spacious market town on the edge of the hill-country between the Clyde and the Tweed.

The Tam o'Shanter Museum, one of Ayr's most popular attractions, is dedicated to the local poet, Robert Burns

Biggar people are remarkably keen on preserving the past, and have created their own Museum Trust.

It runs the Gladstone Court Museum — a splendid re-creation, using the original shop-fronts, of the grocer's, chemist's, ironmonger's, bootmaker's and so on which used to serve the town; a Heritage Centre in the mid-Victorian Moat Park Church; and Greenhill, a historic farmhouse re-erected in a riverside park to provide an exhibition on the Covenanters.

Even the gasworks, which closed in the 1970s after being at work for more than 130 years, is now an out-station of the Royal Scottish Museum in Edinburgh.

BIGGAR is on the A702, 29 miles south of Edinburgh.

BUTE
Argyll and Bute

After Arran, this is the biggest of the islands in the Firth of Clyde; but it is very different in appearance. The appeal of Bute is not in mountains, but in a fine variety of low hills, rolling farmland, open moorlands and attractive woods.

Rothesay, the island town, has been one of the favourite Clyde Coast holiday resorts since the days when the steamers began operating.

Here and in other parts of the island there are facilities for golf, bowling, tennis, fishing, diving, swimming and pony-trekking. Rothesay Bay and Kames Bay, to the north, are good sailing centres.

Rothesay is a mainly Victorian town which was built round its extensive bay.

There are walks to the north-west in the Skeoch Wood, and again to the north-east in Bogany Wood, which is planted on the side of Canada Hill — so-called because it was from here

that the people left behind had their last glimpse of the sailing-ships taking emigrants to a new life in North America.

In happier days, Canada Hill remains an excellent viewpoint over the Firth of Clyde and the mainland hills. Rothesay's golf course, designed by the great James Braid, sweeps towards the summit. The motorist's way to it is up through the hairpin bends of the well-named Serpentine Road.

The Bute Museum on Rothesay's Chapelhill has comprehensive displays on the island's history, archaeology and wildlife.

Nearby is the most imposing historic building on Bute — the partly

A taste of bygone days is preserved at Biggar

Pony-trekking is popular along Bute's pebbly shores

restored 13th-century Rothesay Castle, standing behind a moat in the very centre of the town.

For over a century it was one of the regular residences of the Scottish kings. In 1398, Robert III created his eldest son Duke of Rothesay. As the present-day heir to the throne, Prince Charles retains that as his principal Scottish title.

Following the main coast road round the foot of Canada Hill — through Craigmore and Orcadia, past the gardens and glasshouses of Ardencraig, and beyond the village of Ascog whose churchyard contains only a single grave — leads to the unexpected sight of Kerrycroy, a hamlet at the entrance to the grounds of Mountstuart, the mid-Victorian mansion of the 6th Marquess of Bute.

The 2nd Marchioness had Kerrycroy built in the style of a typical English estate village, complete with half-timbered cottages round a maypole.

There is another holiday resort village at Kilchattan Bay on the south-east coast. Sandy bays are strung along the west coast at Dunagoil, Stravanan, Scalpsie and Ettrick.

And the depression which runs diagonally across the centre of Bute accommodates a line of open waterways — the Kirk Dam, Loch Fad and Loch Quien — which point directly at the mountain peaks of Arran, only one of many superb views on this beautiful and varied island.

⛴ *THE CAR-FERRY TO ROTHESAY sails from Wemyss Bay on the A78. A smaller car-ferry to Rhubodach at the north end of the island leaves from Colintraive on the A886.*

CLYDE-MUIRSHIEL REGIONAL PARK
Inverclyde/Renfrew/Cunninghame

Covering 30,000 acres in public and private ownership — lochs, glens, woodlands, high sheep farms and grouse moors — this 'park' is left mostly in its entirely natural state.

There are four major access points, each with its own information centre and each with a quite different appeal.

Cornalees Bridge is on the outflow from the Loch Thom scheme of reservoirs and 'cuts' — or open channels — which supplied water to the houses, mills and factories of Greenock from 1827 until the cuts were made redundant in 1971.

Now the area is a preserved industrial monument; but there is also a great deal of wildlife interest around the moorland tracks which follow the cuts to high-level viewpoints over the Firth of Clyde.

Muirshiel is an old estate in the lonely headwaters of the River Calder. Surrounded by grouse moors, it has woodland trails and a series of rocky waterfalls.

Lower down, Castle Semple Loch has been turned into a recreational area for rowers, dinghy-sailors, canoeists and coarse anglers who fish for pike, perch and roach.

At one time a part of Castle Semple Loch, Aird Meadow was then drained in an effort to transform it into arable land; but it has now gone back to marsh, and is a reserve of the Royal Society for the Protection of Birds.

There are ground-level observation hides on the edge of scrubby woodland and a visitor centre with a first-floor viewing area over a habitat which attracts more than 100 species of resident and migrant wildfowl.

🚗 *CORNALEES BRIDGE is 3 miles east of Inverkip on the A78. Muirshiel is 4 miles north-west of Lochwinnoch on the B786. Castle Semple Loch and Aird Meadow are immediately east of Lochwinnoch.*

CULZEAN COUNTRY PARK
Kyle and Carrick

If Clyde-Muirshiel is left largely in its natural state, Culzean is a park of an entirely different character. It is a one-time private estate on which generations of landowners lavished attention: more than 500 acres of woodlands and shoreline centred on a glorious Adam castle on a clifftop overlooking the Firth of Clyde.

Culzean Castle, built in the second half of the 18th century for the Earls of Cassillis, was offered to the National Trust for Scotland in 1945 by their successor as head of the Kennedy family, the 5th Marquess of Ailsa.

The Trust still owns the castle, while the grounds form a Country Park managed by it for various local authorities.

Guided tours of the castle show off its impeccable furnishings and spectacular architectural details, like the superb oval staircase and the round drawing room high above the sea.

Many of the original plans of the castle, and information on the running of the estate through the years, are on show in the Park Centre which has been created by the restoration of Robert Adam's stylish but practical Home Farm complex.

Reminders of the spacious days when Culzean was a genuinely stately home are ornamental features in the grounds like the Orangery, the Camellia House, the Fountain Court, the swan pond, aviary and walled garden.

But there are many purpose-built features too: a bath house and ice house, the estate's own gas house, a fire pond, pathways originally in-

Red deer, although a rare species, can still be spotted at Culzean

tended for gamekeepers and laundrymaids hurrying about their work.

The beautiful and varied woodlands are criss-crossed by footpaths. Others follow the clifftops and descend to secluded beaches. And a series of sea-caves bite deep into the sandstone cliffs.

CULZEAN is on the A719, 13 miles south-west of Ayr.

GIRVAN
Kyle and Carrick

Looking directly out across the Firth of Clyde to the huge, isolated rock of Ailsa Craig, Girvan is a holiday resort with a long sandy beach, sports facilities and entertainments.

But it is also a fishing port with an attractive riverside harbour where gulls racket around as catches are being landed.

Ten miles offshore, Ailsa Craig appears from this angle to be virtually sheer-sided. But Girvan boat-hirers take parties to the island.

Only lighthouse-keepers occupy it now, but there is plenty to see from the steep, zig-zag path which starts from the derelict gas-works beside the lighthouse, passes a small ruined castle and then climbs dizzily above it to the 1110-ft summit.

The 360-degree view is magnificent, taking in the coast of Ireland, Kintyre and the Galloway Hills, and the island peaks of Arran and Jura.

Bird-watchers will also be impressed by the traffic of gannets around their fishing grounds in the Firth from the thousands of nests on the southern and western cliffs of Ailsa Craig itself.

GIRVAN is on the A77, 22 miles south of Ayr.

GREAT CUMBRAE
Cunninghame

This is an island to which generations of holidaymakers have returned year after year. The inland hills are partly given over to sheep and dairy-farming, while the 11-mile coast road passes a Marine Biological Station open to the public, the massive lava dyke known as the Lion Rock, the National Water Sports Training Centre and — on the west coast facing across the Firth of Clyde to the island of Bute — red-sandstone inlets where shelduck gather, and a beautiful beach at Fintray Bay.

An 'inner circle' road leads to the Glaid Stone, Cumbrae's highest point at 415 ft, below which stretches a well laid-out golf course.

The only town on the island is Millport, spreading for two miles round a semi-circular bay with a cluster of rocky points and islets. The Garrison, originally built by the captain of an 18th-century revenue cutter, houses the Museum of the Cumbraes.

One of many pleasant walks is along the ridge of the Farland Hills which shelter Millport from the easterly winds — especially on a clear evening when, beyond the lights of the town and of the yachts and cruisers anchored in the bay, the sun sets over the mountain peaks of Arran.

THE CAR-FERRY for Cumbrae sails from Largs on the A78.

HAMILTON
Hamilton

This sprawling town above the south bank of the Clyde is a place with a very long history, mentioned under its original name of Cadzow in accounts of events in the 6th century.

Robert the Bruce gave the lands of Cadzow to the Hamilton family, and a royal charter of 1445 later changed the town's name to theirs.

On the outskirts is the extraordinary mausoleum completed in 1854 for the 10th Duke of Hamilton. Guided tours allow demonstrations of the remarkably long-lasting echo inside its towering dome.

In its historic core, Hamilton retains some other impressive buildings. Hamilton Museum was originally a 17th-century coaching inn.

Nearby, a Victorian riding school has been transformed into a museum

A thriving fishing industry means that Girvan does not have to depend on tourism alone for its income

Robert Burns

Burns had a love life of almost unravellable complications. In mellow reflection on his passions, he wrote some of the world's gentlest and longest-enduring love songs.

After his first book of poems was published in 1786, he took the sophisticated literary society of Edinburgh by storm. But one glowing review contained the millstone-round-the-neck phrase 'heaven-sent ploughman'.

Burns was in fact a well-educated and well-read tenant farmer; a lively conversationalist with a quick if often outrageous turn of speech and actions.

Memories of literary conversations fade quickly. Raffish behaviour can hardly establish a long-term reputation. Love songs are not entirely the

It says a great deal about Lowland Scots that the towering personality they recognise above all others is not a politician or a general or an industrialist — but a poet.

Robert Burns, dead almost 200 years, retains an enthusiastic and affectionate following, not only in Scotland but also in every continent where Scots have settled.

The anniversary of his birth in 1759 — 25 January — is celebrated all over the world in traditional-style Burns Suppers; and that date is referred to in Scotland, as a matter of course, as Burns Night.

Robert Burns was born in this whitewashed cottage in Alloway (*above*). He and his wife Jean rented a room in this house at Mauchline (*below*), now a museum

stuff of immortality.

But Burns was also a liberal, crusader and annihilating satirist. *Holy Willie's Prayer* and *Address to the Deil* savaged the ultra-conservatives in the 18th-century Scottish church as no amount of pamphlet-writing or speechifying could have done. Away from disputations, he created in *Tam O'Shanter* the fastest-moving and most uproarious of Scottish ballads.

Burns was in tune with the early ideals of the French Revolution. And part of his lasting appeal is that, in poems like *A Man's a Man for A' That*, he delivered some of the most powerful declarations of equality ever written.

It sums him up that, in every Burns Supper throughout the world, although one toast is 'To the Lassies', the main speaker of the evening proposes his 'Immortal Memory'.

of the Cameronians — the locally-raised regiment formed from the ranks of the Covenanters after the Glorious Revolution of 1688 ended their half-century of relentless persecution.

East of the town there is a country park split by the winding and thickly-wooded Avon Gorge. On one side of the river is the ruin of the Hamiltons' old stronghold of Cadzow Castle.

On the other side is Chatelherault, a restored 18th-century hunting lodge in the grand style. The Dukes of Hamilton are also the Dukes of Chatelherault in France.

HAMILTON is off the M74, south-east of Glasgow.

IRVINE
Cunninghame

As one of Scotland's New Towns, Irvine has its fair share of industrial development, bypass roads and up-to-date recreational facilities — both indoors and outdoors, notably at the multi-million pound Magnum Centre and the Beach Park around it.

But Irvine also pays great attention to the past. The old harbour area on the river is being rebuilt as the Scottish Maritime Museum; and Irvine Burns Club is one of the most important in the world, with an irreplaceable collection of documents, paintings, and rare first editions.

The club has also been closely involved with the restoration of the Glasgow Vennel, the street where Burns's efforts as a young man to make a trade out of flax-dressing were frustrated by the 'scoundrel of the first water' his partner turned out to be, and by 'the drunken carelessness of my partner's wife', who started a fire which gutted the shop during her New Year carousings in 1782.

Dean Castle Country Park, Kilmarnock, lies amid a 200-acre estate

However, it was in Irvine that Burns was first advised to think about publishing his poems, and here that he discovered the works of Robert Fergusson, whom he regarded for the rest of his life as his poetic mentor.

IRVINE is 11 miles north of Ayr.

KILBARCHAN
Renfrew

In 1723 the Bryden family built themselves a cottage in the heart of this weavers' village; and the same house, still with the Brydens' initials carved on the lintel, is carefully preserved as a museum, not simply of the long-since abandoned handloom-weaving trade, but also of the furniture, furnishings, clothes and domestic equipment of generations gone by.

The Weaver's Cottage is now in the hands of the National Trust for Scotland, and a working loom has been re-installed in the ground-floor workshop where generations of Brydens, Brodies and Christies bent to their shuttles.

KILBARCHAN is off the A761, 5 miles west of Paisley.

KILMARNOCK
Kilmarnock and Loudoun

Always a rival to Ayr, Kilmarnock is the industrial centre of what used to be the county of Ayrshire, and the home of one of the world's best-known brands of Scotch whisky.

The town played a very important part in the life of Robert Burns, because in 1786 the local printer John Wilson produced the first — 'Kilmarnock' — edition of his *Poems, Chiefly in the Scottish Dialect*.

Wilson's printing shop has gone, but its site is marked by a plaque in the town's shopping centre.

There is a Burns Memorial in the

Kay Park, but Kilmarnock is better known for the Dean Castle Country Park — 200 acres of woods and farmland where the Fenwick and Craufurdland Waters meet. It is centred on the basically 14th-century castle of the Boyd family, which features collections of musical instruments and tapestries, and a well-presented medieval armoury.

KILMARNOCK is off the A77, 21 miles south of Glasgow.

LARGS
Cunninghame

One of the most significant encounters in Scottish history took place at Largs in 1263. Alexander III, having failed in negotiations with the Vikings, defeated their battle fleet here. They gave up control of all the Hebrides, holding on for a few years more only to Orkney and Shetland.

With enthusiastic Norwegian help, Largs celebrates the occasion every September with a Viking Festival of sports, parades, bonfires and music.

Largs is a well-equipped holiday resort on the Firth of Clyde, with facilities for all kinds of sports from windsurfing to golf. The most prominent of its open spaces is Douglas Park, which begins among formal gardens in the town itself and sweeps uphill to a magnificent viewpoint over the Firth and its islands.

Back down among the shoppers and visitors, a little lane off the main street leads to the sole remaining aisle of the old parish church.

Maintained as an ancient monument, the Skelmorlie Aisle contains the Renaissance-style tomb built in 1636 for the Montgomeries of Skelmorlie, and its barrel-vaulted ceiling retains the original painted scenes, emblems and Zodiacal signs.

South of the town, Kelburn Castle is the home of the Earl of Glasgow, whose family have been here since the 12th century. Its extensive grounds, on both sides of the fine ravine where the Kel Burn cascades over waterfalls, are now a Country Centre, with winding paths through woodlands of beech and ash, oak, sycamore, chestnut, birch and spruce.

LARGS is on the A78, 30 miles north of Ayr.

LANARK
Clydesdale

At the foot of the busy High Street, Lanark Cross is the focus of interest in this market town in the heart of Covenanter country. Its history goes back to a royal charter, now lost but believed to have been signed by David II at Lanark Castle in 1140.

William Wallace, Bruce's predecessor in the independence wars of the 13th and 14th centuries, had a house near the Cross. And this is where the Lanimer Week celebrations come to an end with the crowning of the Lanimer Queen.

To the east, Lanark Moor is the town's historic common land. The racecourse here has, sadly, been given up for regular events; but the moor is still parkland, with woods, a loch and an excellent golf course.

A side-road in the town leads to what is probably Scotland's grandest industrial monument — the village of New Lanark, established in the 1780s where the water-power of the River Clyde would turn the machinery of its cotton mills.

Although the last mill closed in 1968, a massive restoration programme has preserved New Lanark as it was in the heyday of Robert

Although a lived-in village New Lanark remains as it was in the time of Robert Owen

Owen's pioneering social experiments; but it is still a lived-in village, and no moribund museum.

From Caithness Row at the east of the village, a nature trail leads up to the wide and rocky Falls of Clyde. Although a hydro-electric power scheme taps most of the water before it tumbles over the Falls, on a few days every year their full majestic flow is restored.

LANARK is 14 miles south-east of Hamilton.

LEADHILLS
Clydesdale

In the 16th century, James V had some sceptical French guests served with 'fruit' from the seemingly barren Lowther Hills — dishes heaped with gold coins.

But the later riches of the Lowthers came from the mineral which gave the remote village of Leadhills its name. It is still lived in, although the last of the mine-workings closed in 1928.

There are memorials to John Taylor, whom the lively upland air allowed to survive until the ripe age of 137, and to William Symington, designer in 1788 of the world's first steamboat engine. And the library of the Leadhills Miners' Reading Society still serves subscribers today, after more than 240 years.

LEADHILLS is on the B797, 6 miles south of Abington.

MAUCHLINE
Cumnock and Doon Valley

This is one of the important stops on the Burns Heritage Trail — the town where many of the characters lambasted in his most famous satires were all too clearly identifiable, but where he also made influential friends, many of whom are buried in the parish churchyard.

The two-storey stone-and-slate house where Burns and his wife Jean Armour first rented a room has been turned into an attractively laid-out museum, and not just on the Burns theme. There are displays on the town's most famous industries — the old Mauchline box-ware much prized by collectors, and the still-in-production curling-stone factory.

To the north, the ornate red-sandstone tower of the National Burns Memorial is a viewpoint over the fields of Mossgiel where the brothers Robert and Gilbert Burns struggled through some difficult years as tenant farmers, and where the poet, one harvest-time, encountered the 'wee, sleekit, cowrin, tim'rous beastie' which figures in *To a Mouse*.

MAUCHLINE is on the A76, 8 miles south of Kilmarnock.

The famous Paisley pattern captivated fashionable 19th-century Europeans

OLD DAILLY
Kyle and Carrick

Time has passed this village by; but it has left the mellowed and well-kept ruin of the original parish church, with its notable Covenanter memorials.

To the east lies the historic estate of Bargany, whose beautiful woodland gardens, around an ornamental lake and down a narrow glen, are open to the public most of the year.

In the hills above Old Dailly, guided tours can be arranged of the astonishing Penkill Castle, lavishly rebuilt and refurnished in Victorian times with paintings, tapestries, murals and architectural details contributed by the Pre-Raphaelite artists who were friends of the laird.

OLD DAILLY is on the B734, 3 miles east of Girvan.

PAISLEY
Renfrew

In 1163 Walter FitzAlan was given a charter to establish a priory near the banks of the White Cart Water. It was soon elevated to the status of an abbey; and through all the changing years Paisley Abbey — now a charge of the Church of Scotland — has remained the dignified centre of the town.

Walter FitzAlan was also David I's hereditary High Steward of Scotland. His successors changed their surname to Stewart and eventually to Stuart.

This was the line which produced the monarchs of Scotland and, later, of the United Kingdom, from Robert II — grandson of Robert the Bruce — to that James VII of Scotland and II of England who abandoned his throne in 1688.

All but one of the original line of High Stewards are buried in the Abbey, which has memorials, wood-carving and stained glass windows of the highest order. And the long years over which it achieved its present form are shown by the progression of architectural styles, from the Romanesque onwards.

The Museum and Art Galleries in the High Street display hundreds of 'Paisley pattern' shawls — based on Kashmiri designs — which were the height of European fashion for much of the 19th century.

Behind the Museum, the Coats Observatory — concerned with satellite weather reports, seismological recordings and general astronomical work — has regular guided tours.

Rising to the south of the town, the road to the 1000-acre Gleniffer Country Park — with its walks, picnic areas and wide-ranging views — was used in Edwardian times as a test hill for the pioneering Arrol-Johnston

All manner of sports and leisure pursuits are practised in the Strathclyde Country Park

cars, and again in the 1920s for the thousands of Beardmore taxis which Paisley sent to the cab-ranks of London and other British cities.

🚗 *PAISLEY is on the A737, west of Glasgow.*

STRATHCLYDE COUNTRY PARK
Motherwell/Hamilton

Occupying the riverside ground between the towns of Motherwell and Hamilton, this recreational area centres on a 200-acre artificial lake beside the Clyde, used for training and competitions in sailing, rowing and canoeing.

On land, there are three main sports pavilions serving football, rugby, hockey and cricket pitches; a golf course; nature trails and other walks to locations like the excavated bath-house built by the Romans.

🚗 *STRATHCLYDE COUNTRY PARK is reached from Junctions 4 and 5 on the M74.*

TROON
Kyle and Carrick

Of all the resorts on the Ayrshire coast, where most things take second place to golf, Troon devotes more space to it than any other. The town is ringed by no fewer than five 18-hole courses and has played host to several Open Championships.

One local hotel has a 'real' — rather than lawn — tennis court; there is an archery club; a riding academy teaches equitation in the classic style; and an extensive marina occupies the old inner harbour, on the curving promontory that reminded the early settlers who gave the place its name of the shape of a nose — for which their word was 'trwyn'.

🚗 *TROON is on the A759, 6 miles north of Ayr.*

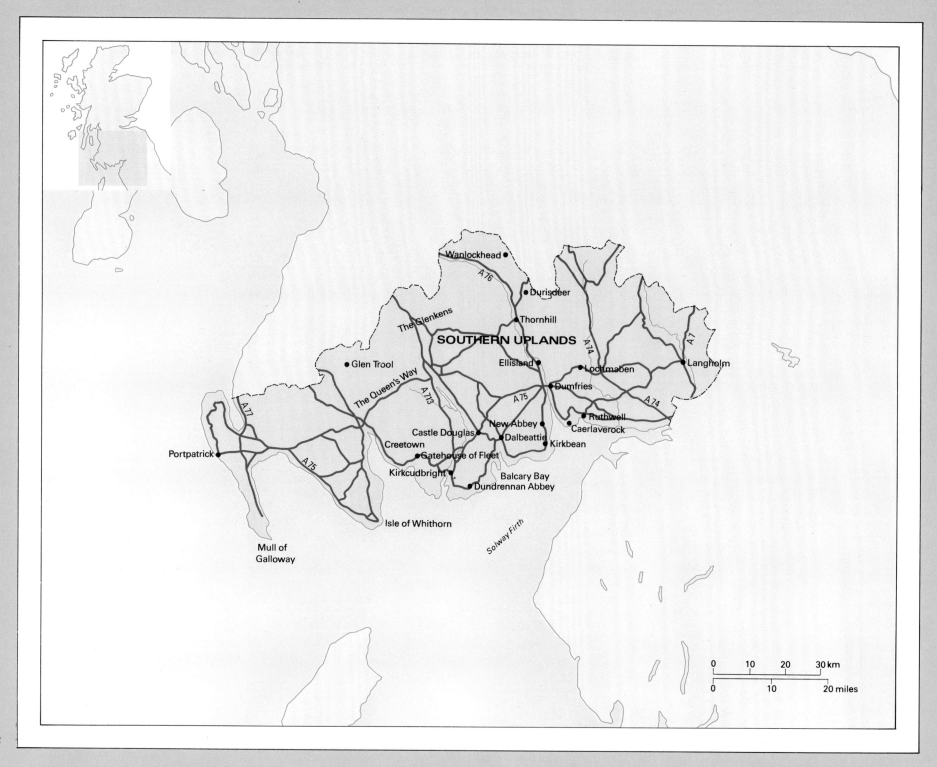

Wanlockhead

A 76

Durisdeer

The Glenkens

Thornhill

SOUTHERN UPLANDS

Glen Trool

Ellisland

A 74

Lochmaben

A 7

Langholm

The Queen's Way

A 713

A 75

Dumfries

A 71

New Abbey

Ruthwell

Castle Douglas

Dalbeattie

Caerlaverock

Creetown

Kirkbean

Gatehouse of Fleet

Portpatrick

A 75

Kirkcudbright

Balcary Bay

Dundrennan Abbey

Isle of Whithorn

A 74

Mull of
Galloway

Solway Firth

0   10   20   30 km

0   10   20 miles

Dumfries & Galloway

High above Loch Trool stands Bruce's Stone, facing the spot where Robert the Bruce defeated the English at Glen Trool

IN LOYAL REMEMBRANCE OF ROBERT THE BRUCE KING OF SCOTS WHOSE VICTORY IN THIS GLEN OVER AN ENGLISH FORCE IN MARCH 1307 OPENED THE CAMPAIGN OF INDEPENDENCE WHICH HE BROUGHT TO A DECISIVE CLOSE AT BANNOCKBURN ON 24TH JUNE 1314

SCOTLAND'S WESTERN BORDER with England is formed by the unobtrusive meanders of the little River Sark, which flows into the head of the Solway Firth. As the Firth progresses and widens, it passes beautiful river estuaries on its way to the daunting cliffs of the Mull of Galloway, where sea-birds wheel around a wave-lashed lighthouse point.

Inland, there are richly farmed parishes with well-wooded estates, notable castles, fine gardens and busy market towns. But on The Moors of Wigtownshire, lowland dairy farms give way to bare peat-mosses where bog-cotton shivers in the breeze.

Galloway Forest Park covers 240 square miles of plantations, lochs and unexpectedly rugged hills; it also has a network of forest trails.

Galloway was the scene of Robert the Bruce's early victories against the occupying English armies. Mary, Queen of Scots spent her last night in Scotland at Dundrennan Abbey, on her way to exile.

Paul Jones, first Commander of the United States Navy, was born a gardener's son at Arbigland. Thomas Telford, the founding father of British civil engineering, was brought up in Glendinning.

And Dumfries is the last resting-place of Robert Burns, who in his later years moved from Ayrshire to be a farmer and revenue-officer in the district where his writings were as various as the stirring *Scots Wha Hae* and the rollicking *Tam o'Shanter*.

BALCARY BAY
Stewartry

One of the smaller inlets in the extensive tidal stretch of Auchencairn Bay, Balcary is one of the most timelessly beautiful places on the Solway Coast. A very old-established stake-net fishery still traps salmon when the tide recedes, and there is a fine view to the one-time smugglers' outpost on Hestan Island, a mile or so offshore.

But the smugglers were active on the mainland too. Balcary Bay Hotel has a bar converted from secret cellars excavated by the smuggling company who built the house in the first place.

A bracing walk leads uphill from the bay, starting on farmland then skimming along the top of sea-bird cliffs before turning round Balcary Point for a view of the Cumberland hills across the wider Solway Firth.

Here, it passes above the natural rock formation called Adam's Chair, from which lantern signals used to be given to contraband ships approaching secretly at night.

BALCARY BAY is 2 miles south-east of Auchencairn on the A711.

CAERLAVEROCK
Nithsdale

On its eastern side, the estuary of the River Nith turns along the ragged inlets and extensive salt-marshes of the Merse, a lonely and atmospheric part of the coast. Behind the Merse, stands one of the most striking castles in Scotland — the red-sandstone ruin of Caerlaverock.

The first castle here was built in the late 13th century, to the elegant triangular plan followed by its successors, with curtain walls between sturdy towers.

Protected by a surrounding earthwork and a moat, Caerlaverock

Caerlaverock Castle, a handsome ruin, once suffered a 13-week siege

was the stronghold of the Maxwell family. In 1640 Robert Maxwell, the 1st Earl of Nithsdale, held the castle for Charles I, but had to surrender it after a 13-week siege by the Covenanters. They partly dismantled it, for the last — but not by any means the first time in its turbulent career.

Beyond the castle, a National Nature Reserve and a Wildfowl Trust reserve cover almost 14,000 acres of salt-marsh and farmland, the winter roost of thousands of pinkfoot and greylag geese, and most of the population of barnacle geese from Spitzbergen.

CAERLAVEROCK is off the B725, 8 miles south-east of Dumfries.

CASTLE DOUGLAS
Stewartry

Originally, this was a village called Carlingwark, sharing its name with the loch on its southern boundary. But in 1792, raised to the status of a burgh, its name was changed to honour the landowner Sir William Douglas.

Castle Douglas grew into a well-planned town which has a famous market for Ayrshire and Galloway cattle. Carlingwark Loch is one of its major recreational features; dinghies sail among wooded islets, and there is a public park on the banks.

Beyond the south-west corner of the loch, the grounds of Threave

House are the National Trust for Scotland's School of Practical Gardening, open to visitors along with a woodland nature trail.

The Trust also owns Threave Wildfowl Refuge, bounded by the River Dee. This is a noted winter roost for migratory ducks and geese.

One of the islands in the Dee is the site of Threave Castle, the ruined but still purposeful four-storey fortress of the Black Douglases, reached by a short boat trip from the east bank.

It was built at the end of the 14th century with double protection against a surprise attack; although the castle is on the edge of its island, a right-angled moat ensures that it is surrounded on all sides by water.

Reached only by boat, Threave Castle is surrounded by a deep, lily-filled moat

Like Caerlaverock, its last military engagement was a successful siege by the Covenanters in 1640.

CASTLE DOUGLAS is on the A75, 18 miles south-west of Dumfries.

CREETOWN
Wigtown

Granite from the quarries near this village at the head of Wigtown Bay was used to build the Thames Embankment in London and the Mersey Docks in Liverpool. Nowadays, on a smaller scale, craft-workers here create jewellery from gold, silver and semi-precious stones, as well as from unusual kinds of wood.

The astonishing Gem Rock Museum houses a unique collection of minerals and gemstones. Among hundreds of these on display are rose quartz, malachite and jade; a massive amethyst geode; a 200 million year-old droplet of water encased in a South American agate; and a remarkable group of apparently dull-hued stones which come to brilliant multi-coloured life under ultra-violet light.

CREETOWN is on the A75, 7 miles south-east of Newton Stewart.

DALBEATTIE
Stewartry

Most of Dalbeattie — houses, churches, the square-towered town hall and the inevitable Queen Victoria Jubilee fountain — is built of granite. And it was the opening in the late 18th century of the huge quarry on Craignair Hill across the River Urr which sparked off the growth of this pleasant town with its variety of parks and open spaces.

Dalbeattie's own port on the Urr could take only shallow-draught vessels; so an old smuggling harbour called Boglescreek, a few miles down the winding course of the river, was enlarged to become the village of Palnackie. For generations, it sent locally-owned ships with cargoes of Dalbeattie granite, not only to British sea-port cities, but also to Scandinavia, Belgium and Portugal.

Down the other bank of the river, beyond the entrance to the trails in Solway Forest, the non-identical twin villages of Kippford and Rockcliffe, linked by a maze of beautiful viewpoint paths, face the almost excessively tidal estuary of the Urr.

Kippford has a long row of former quarrymen's, boatbuilders' and fishermen's cottages, and is the headquarters of the Solway Yacht Club.

Rockcliffe's villas among well-tended gardens look out over the sands and rocky outcrops which made it a favourite 19th-century bathing resort.

🚗 *DALBEATTIE is on the A711, 14 miles south-west of Dumfries.*

DUMFRIES
Nithsdale

Built along both sides of the winding River Nith, Dumfries was created a royal burgh as early as 1186, and it remains the largest town in Dumfries and Galloway.

Many historic events have been recorded here. In 1306 Robert the Bruce killed Sir John Comyn, representative of the English King Edward I, in the Greyfriars church, and committed himself to the independence war which ended in victory eight long years later.

Dumfries was only passively involved in the Jacobite Risings — because this was no Jacobite town. Bonnie Prince Charlie occupied it for three days in December 1745; but at that time, despite its up-river situation, Dumfries was far more in-

The Globe Inn, Dumfries, is full of Burns memorabilia

terested in developing its sea-going trade.

This was one of the reasons why Robert Burns moved to Dumfries in 1791: to devote himself wholeheartedly to his flourishing Excise career, as well as to the writing of the hundreds of songs which were the great creative output of his later years.

His second residence in the town showed how he was prospering — a solid, two-storey house in local sandstone.

In the summer of 1796, however, Burns took seriously ill. A doctor friend gave the fatal advice to try a sea-bathing cure in the Solway, which simply accelerated the condition.

He died at home in Dumfries, on 21 July. Two army regiments and a procession of thousands of mourners accompanied him to his last resting-place in St Michael's churchyard.

The Burns House, where his wife Jean outlived him by no fewer than 38 years, is now a well cared-for museum.

The main Dumfries Museum, however, is a larger and very well equipped one on higher ground. It began life as an 18th-century windmill, and the top of the old windmill tower houses a camera obscura, which still gives an intriguing outlook over activity down in the town.

🚗 *DUMFRIES is on the A75, 25 miles west of Gretna.*

DUNDRENNAN ABBEY
Stewartry

Very little is known of this substantial but out-of-the-way Cistercian house from its founding in 1142 until the May evening in 1568 when it finally entered the mainstream of Scottish history.

Mary, Queen of Scots, having abdicated her throne, spent her last night on Scottish soil here. Next morning, she took a ship across the Solway Firth from the little natural

harbour now called Port Mary.

But exile in Queen Elizabeth's England was no safer for the woman who was, after all, next in succession to *that* throne. Elizabeth had her cousin held under house arrest for 19 years, and then ordered her execution.

Dundrennan is now a gracious ancient monument. Major parts of the cloister, the chapter-house and the abbey church are still standing. Among its many memorials is a mystery not mentioned in any surviving records — the carving of an unidentified abbot, quite clearly stabbed to death.

🚗 *DUNDRENNAN is on the A711, 12 miles south-west of Dalbeattie.*

DURISDEER
Nithsdale

There are traces of ancient earthworks on the Lowther Hills above the tiny village of Durisdeer, and the line of an 18th-century coaching road can be followed through a pass to the north-east, on the same route up the rounded, heathery, sheep-grazed slopes.

The parish church, standing back from a noisy rookery, was probably built — according to a sundial above the south door — in 1699.

It attracts particular interest because of the mausoleum, completed a few years later, for the 2nd Duke and Duchess of Queensberry. A Dutch sculptor created this 'exuberant monument' in black and white marble.

🚗 *DURISDEER is off the A702, 6 miles north of Thornhill.*

ELLISLAND
Nithsdale

This is the farm, by the banks of the Nith, where Robert Burns settled

when he first moved from Ayrshire to Dumfries-shire. He took it over in March 1788, and found out all too soon that the land was virtually exhausted.

Once he started with the Excise — in September 1789 — he had the triple task of riding all over the county on official business, continuing to write, and overseeing work on the farm.

He left Ellisland after three and a half hard years; but it was here that he composed the magnificent ballad *Tam o'Shanter*, set in the Alloway of his boyhood.

His wife said that he wrote the entire poem in a single day, walking by the riverside, acting all the parts, and roaring with laughter as his imagination took hilarious wing.

ELLISLAND is off the A76, 6 miles north-west of Dumfries.

GATEHOUSE OF FLEET
Stewartry

Within a one-mile radius of the bridge over the River Fleet at Gatehouse there is enough to keep any enquiring visitor happily occupied for weeks.

This fascinating little town was laid out towards the end of the 18th century as a centre for cotton-milling. Many buildings from its heyday survive — not only elegant Georgian houses, but also others long since converted from their original use: as a mill, perhaps, a tannery, a brass-foundry, a soap-works or a brewery.

It was the landowner James Murray of Cally who engineered the expansion of the town. The old Cally estate parkland is now mostly in the hands of the Forestry Commission.

Fleet Forest Nursery has operated here since 1936, raising millions of

Cardoness Castle stands on high ground at Gatehouse of Fleet

Bruce's Stone stands high above Loch Trool in Galloway Forest Park

conifer seedlings; but there are trails through broad-leaved woodland.

Robert Burns, inevitably, came this way. It was in the Murray Arms at Gatehouse, following a long and drizzly moorland ride, that he put on paper the words of the song *Scots Wha Hae* — his stirring version of Robert the Bruce's address to his army before the Battle of Bannockburn.

The part-restored 15th-century Cardoness Castle stands on a hilltop above the Creetown road. For generations, the McCullochs of Cardoness were notorious for their hair-trigger tempers. The murder of a neighbour gave one of them the distinction of being almost the last man to submit to the attentions of the 'maiden' — the euphemistic name for the old Scottish guillotine.

GATEHOUSE OF FLEET is 14 miles south-west of Castle Douglas.

64

Irish pilgrims were drawn to St Ninian's shrine at Whithorn

GLEN TROOL
Wigtown

In the heart of the Galloway Forest Park, this is a valley which becomes progressively more dramatic until, around Loch Trool, towering hillsides and rugged heathery crags signal the start of the hill-walkers' tracks to the Merrick — at 2764 ft the highest point in Galloway — and the harshly-named, remote upland features like the Rig of the Jarkness and the Murder Hole of Loch Neldricken.

The start of the glen is at the rocky Falls of Minnoch, where forest trails meander through larch and spruce.

There are more than conifer plantations at the head of Loch Trool: the Buchan and Gairland Burns cascade through protected oakwoods.

High above the loch, the finest easily accessible viewpoint is the commemorative Bruce's Stone. Another trail across the hillside opposite shows where an English force, one day in 1307, was ambushed by a barrage of tumbling boulders, behind which Bruce's men rampaged down the hill to clinch the battle known as the Steps of Trool.

GLEN TROOL is north-east of Bargrennan on the A714.

THE GLENKENS
Stewartry

This is the name of the valley where, among lochs and forested hills, the Water of Deugh joins the Water of Ken and the united river combines with the Dee.

Carsphairn, the highest village, had the misfortune to be on the estates of Sir Robert Grierson, whose enthusiastic persecution of Covenanters centred on his own tenants.

There are Covenanter memories too at St John's Town of Dalry, a

The Solway Smugglers

Many things combined to make the Solway Coast the main centre of Scotland's flourishing 18th and 19th-century smuggling trade.

It was within overnight sailing distance of the Isle of Man, where cargoes could be landed quite legally from foreign ports without any duty being paid — and then, quite illegally, trans-shipped to secret mainland harbours, with which the Solway was remarkably well supplied.

This began as a small-scale operation. But then, in 1707, the Union of Parliaments brought Scotland, England and Wales under one central government which at first created, and then greatly increased, the duty payable on imports of wines, spirits, salt, tobacco, lace and other luxury fabrics.

Smuggling activity on the Solway followed suit. Natural sea-caves and specially extended farmhouse cellars were turned into contraband stores. Individual smuggling companies were set up, with their own shareholders, carefully-kept accounts, pony-trains for overland transport, and a network of middle-men in the cities.

It was only in 1822 that the government turned its full attention towards stamping out the illegal trade.

Money was poured into the revenue service — for coastguard stations, patrol boats and greatly increased manpower. New laws brought in much stricter penalties. Within the decade, smuggling had been virtually wiped out.

It has left one highly popular song — not, oddly enough, about the smugglers, but about their pursuers.

When Robert Burns, to help boost his meagre income from farming and from his notoriously tight-fisted Edinburgh publisher, took up his post as a revenue officer, one of the incidents in which he was involved was the capture of an armed smuggling ship, grounded near the mouth of the River Sark.

While waiting impatiently for reinforcements before boarding the ship, he composed a lively song which is still performed in concerts all over Scotland — *The Deil's Awa' wi' the Exciseman*.

bright and attractive hillside village which has its own lively summer street fair; at nearby Balmaclellan, where the 18th-century stonemason Robert Paterson, who travelled the country keeping Covenanter memorials in good condition, gave Sir Walter Scott the idea for 'Old Mortality'; and across the Water of Ken at New Galloway, a trim little town which was once the smallest of Scotland's royal burghs.

The chain of lochs in the Glenkens — Kendoon, Carsfad, Earlstoun and Ken — are all part of the ingenious Galloway hydro-electric scheme opened in 1936.

Its layout and operation are explained in guided tours of the main Tongland power station, nearer the mouth of the Dee, which also has a 29-pool salmon ladder tackled by as many as 4000 fish per year, on their way to the spawning grounds.

◄ THE MAIN ROAD through the Glenkens is the A713 from Ayr to Castle Douglas.

ISLE OF WHITHORN
Wigtown

The first cargo attracted to this little landing-place on the Solway were Irish pilgrims on their way to St Ninian's shrine at Whithorn. A ruined chapel on the island, built specially for them, dates from the 12th century.

As the inland town of Whithorn increased in importance, 'the Isle' was designated as its port. Later, it was the scene of hair-raising escapades in the heyday of the Solway smugglers.

The tidal bar which linked the island to the mainland eventually had houses and a main street built along it. The grassy Isle, with its tiny rock-flanked bays, has become a very attractive, natural public park, centred on an old tide-signalling tower.

The rugged coastline around the Solway is full of caves

Although there are still some fishing boats at Isle of Whithorn, it is now better known as a holiday resort with a flourishing sailing club.

ISLE OF WHITHORN is on the A750, 14 miles south of Wigtown.

KIRKBEAN
Nithsdale

On the edge of the Solwayside farmlands, this is a neatly laid out village where a lane leads over a burn to the parish church built in 1776.

That was a significant date in Kirkbean, as elsewhere: when the American War of Independence broke out, a local sea captain who had emigrated to Virginia was already the 'father' of the fledgling United States Navy.

Although he has gone down in history as Paul Jones, he was born John Paul, son of the gardener on the nearby Arbigland estate.

The church has a memorial font donated in his honour by officers and men of the modern U.S. Navy; and his boyhood home — a cottage at Arbigland — has been visited by many famous Americans.

Not many of them, perhaps, knew that after the war, having failed in his efforts to set up a fur-trading company, he accepted a pressing invitation from Catherine the Great and became a Rear-Admiral in the Russian Black Sea Fleet.

The modern gardens of Arbigland are open to the public for part of the year, sheltering in woodlands back from the secluded Solway shore.

KIRKBEAN is on the A710, 12 miles south of Dumfries.

KIRKCUDBRIGHT
Stewartry

Under both his names, Paul Jones paid separate official visits to the

Kirkbean is an attractive village on the edge of farmland. Nearby is the birthplace of Paul Jones

spacious county town.

The first was when — as John Paul — he stood trial on a vague and quickly-dismissed charge of killing a seaman.

The other was when, commanding a United States warship, he landed a raiding party to try to kidnap the Earl of Selkirk from his estate outside the town.

Jones had a plan — which turned out successfully — to exchange Americans held prisoner in Britain for hostages taken during his coastal raids; but the Earl of Selkirk, away

from home at the time, was not to be one of them.

Paul Jones's Point on St Mary's Isle is a reminder of that bold attempt; just as the bay called Manxman's Lake recalls the contraband cargoes landed from the Isle of Man.

Robert Burns visited Kirkcudbright too, and it was here that he composed the Selkirk Grace with which every Burns Supper begins.

However, this was an important place long before their time. Its name is a corruption of 'the Kirk of (Saint) Cuthbert', established in the 9th

century.

Much of the town is 18th and 19th-century, but its most notable building is the ruined MacLellan's Castle, completed in 1582 and now an ancient monument standing in gardens near the riverside harbour.

The fine Georgian-style Broughton House contains the library and picture collection bequeathed to the town, like the house itself, by the painter Edward Hornel. One of the leaders of Kirkcudbright's artists' colony, he died in 1933.

A gallery beside the harbour shows

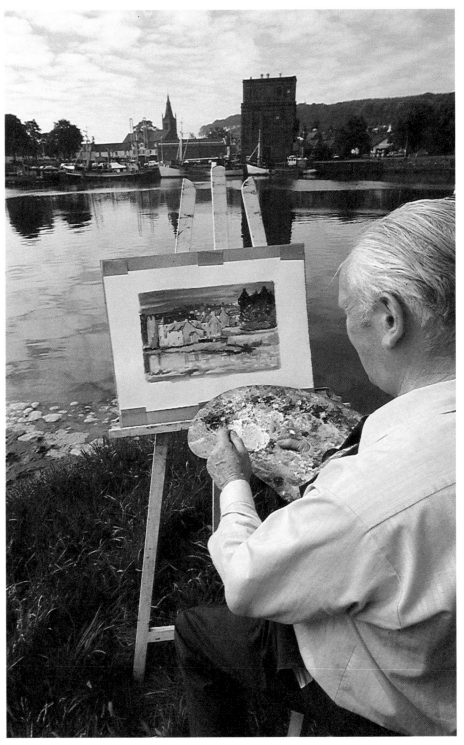

**Kirkcudbright, on the Dee
estuary, is an artist's haven**

that the town's long-standing artistic tradition continues.

KIRKCUDBRIGHT is on the A711, 10 miles south-west of Castle Douglas.

LANGHOLM
Annandale and Eskdale

Located in a valley where, within a quarter of a mile, the Ewes and the Wauchope Waters both join the Border Esk, Langholm is a place with an abundance of riverside walks. Others contour the hills through gentle woodland.

Whita Hill rises steeply to the east. The monument on its 1162-ft summit is a glorious viewpoint — in clear weather, to as far away as the hazy silhouette of the Isle of Man. And an exuberant charge up Whita Hill is one of the features of Langholm's famous Common Riding.

Horses are important around Langholm. So is rugby. And so is the trout and salmon angling on the Esk, the Ewes and the Wauchope.

This has been a significant textile town for something like 200 years. And one local company weaves the most expensive pure-wool suitings in the world.

Langholm also has an extra-terrestrial connection. Its burgh charter dates from the 1620s, but the town took a very long time about deciding who should be dignified by being created its first freeman.

Eventually, in 1972, the choice fell, not on a Langholm man, but on a descendant of Langholm men — Neil Armstrong, the first astronaut to walk on the moon.

LANGHOLM is on the A7, 23 miles south of Hawick.

LOCHMABEN
Annandale and Eskdale

At the head of the main street in Lochmaben there is a statue of Robert the Bruce; and the Latin motto of the little town is *E nobis Liberator Rex* — 'from us is sprung the liberator King.'

His exact birthplace is uncertain, but the Bruce connection with Lochmaben started in 1124, when David I made a grant of lands in Annandale to the Norman family then called de Brus. However, it was only around 1200 that they built a castle in Lochmaben, which survives as a grassy mound on the golf course.

Thanks to its status as the headquarters of the Warden of the Western Marches, Lochmaben suffered badly in the interminable border wars after Robert the Bruce's time. But there were other violent clashes between two great rival families — the Johnstones and the Maxwells — for the wardenship itself.

In 1593 a party of Johnstones had the upper hand in a skirmish at Lochmaben. The Maxwells fled for sanctuary to the parish church, which the Johnstones promptly burned down around them. More Maxwells gathered to have a final showdown with their enemies. By the River Dryfe, east of the town, in the last great family battle, the Maxwells were heavily defeated.

Clan warfare was certainly not confined to the Highlands.

Partly because of the attention it received during these years, the second Lochmaben Castle is little more than a fragmentary ruin on a peninsula at the south end of Castle Loch.

This very attractive heart-shaped loch — one of a remarkable number in and around Lochmaben — is fringed by woodland and forms the centrepiece of a carefully managed

67

nature reserve. There is a dinghy club, and anglers come for the coarse fishing.

Lochmaben is also the home water of that rarest of Scottish freshwater fish, the vendace — still not quite extinct, although a rumoured conservation project has a discreet veil of silence drawn around it.

◢ *LOCHMABEN is on the A709, 10 miles north-east of Dumfries.*

MULL OF GALLOWAY
Wigtown

The 'Land's End' of Galloway is a spectacular headland ringed with seabird cliffs plunging down towards the circling currents where the Solway Firth meets the Irish Sea.

Lichens, wildflowers, close-cropped grazing land and intrusive veins of other rocks streaked through the Mull's basic sandstone all combine to make it an unexpectedly colourful if often windswept place.

Mull of Galloway lighthouse, completed in 1830, is a phenomenal viewpoint. On a fine day, the view extends from the Isle of Man and the Antrim coast to the Inner Hebridean peaks of Jura.

A network of loop roads means that several different routes can be chosen to and from the Mull. They pass through the old smuggling village of Drummore on Luce Bay; the higher-set village of Kirkmaiden with its viewpoint church; and Port Logan, where the wind-driven sea dashes into an exposed west-facing bay.

Before 1800, the laird of Logan had a tidal fish pond built, stocked with cod to provide a regular supply of fish for the mansion house kitchens; but the fish soon became pets, and their successors can still be seen enjoying their hand-feeding today.

The weather in this part of Galloway is surprisingly mild. With walled and wooded areas to divert the wind, many sub-tropical plants can be grown out of doors. Logan Botanic Garden is one of the most famous in Scotland, with dazzling displays of Southern Hemisphere trees and flowering shrubs.

◢ *MULL OF GALLOWAY lighthouse is 5 miles south of Drummore on the A716.*

NEW ABBEY
Nithsdale

The important point about this intriguing and attractive village, which follows a winding main street beyond a bridge over the burn known as the New Abbey Pow, is that its abbey was 'new' only in the context of the 13th century.

It was endowed after her husband's death in 1268 by Devorgilla, widow of the enormously wealthy land-owner John Balliol, and herself the descendant of Scottish kings.

For the 21 years that she survived him, Devorgilla kept constantly by her a little ivory and silver casket which contained her husband's embalmed heart. It was buried with her, when she was laid at rest beside him, before the altar of what its Cistercian monks — who had come from the 'old' abbey at Dundrennan — gave its present name of Sweetheart Abbey.

Only the precinct wall and the abbey kirk, a handsome if ruined building of red sandstone with pointed Gothic arches, remain as an ancient monument; but New Abbey has several other features of note.

The whitewashed 18th-century corn mill, in commercial production until World War II, has been restored and is now open to the public.

And the Victorian mansion-house

The lonely sentinel of Mull of Galloway lighthouse is a stunning viewpoint

of Shambellie, one of David Bryce's Scottish Baronial designs with tower and turrets and skyline crow-stepped gables, has become the Museum of Costume, combining an extensive private collection with other displays from the stock of the Royal Scottish Museum in Edinburgh.

NEW ABBEY is on the A710, 6 miles south of Dumfries.

PORTPATRICK
Wigtown

Named for St Patrick, this very pleasantly situated village has crescents of colour-washed houses half-circling a harbour set in an otherwise cliff-bound coast, with villas and hotels in spacious grounds rising above.

Until mid-Victorian times, it was the ferry-port for the short sea crossing to Donaghadee in Ireland, made redundant only by the development of the rival port of Stranraer. Portpatrick used to have both town and harbour stations.

Colonel Street and Barrack Street recall that this was where troops embarked for postings in Ireland; and some buildings date from the harbour extension work started in the 1820s.

Present-day Portpatrick is a colourful and well equipped holiday resort. A flight of steps up the North Cliff marks the start of the 212-mile coast-to-coast Southern Upland Way, which begins as a familiar village walk alongside the high-level golf course, before heading north-east across Wigtownshire towards Glen Trool.

PORTPATRICK is on the A77, 8 miles south-west of Stranraer.

Portpatrick is a pleasant and lively holiday village encircling a harbour, once the crossing point to Ireland

THE QUEEN'S WAY
Wigtown and Stewartry

This stretch of road through the Galloway Forest Park was named by the Forestry Commission at the time of the Queen's silver jubilee in 1978.

It passes a memorial to another of Robert the Bruce's early victories — this time at the skirmish of Moss Raploch in 1307; the very informative Galloway Deer Museum, which also includes displays on the geology and botany of the Park, as well as modern stained-glass windows on wildlife themes; a hillside red deer enclosure and a similar wild goat park; and the start of the summer-only Raiders Road forest drive alongside the Black Water of Dee, on a route followed by 18th-century cattle rustlers hurrying back from raids on Solway estates.

The finest scenery on the Queen's Way is at Talnotry, where forested hills rise sharply to a monument in honour of Alexander Murray, a locally-born shepherd's son who became one of the most notable Oriental linguists in early 19th-century Europe.

There are fine waterfalls at Talnotry, and a stiff four-mile forest trail which rises to extensive hilltop viewpoints and the site of old lead and nickel mines beside an abandoned 17th-century coaching road.

🚗 *THE QUEEN'S WAY is part of the A712, west of New Galloway.*

RUTHWELL
Nithsdale

In farmlands a mile back from the Solway, this neat village of 18th and 19th-century cottages is notable because of the activities of a remarkable parish minister, the Reverend Dr. Henry Duncan, who served here from 1799.

He was a man of many parts —

The richly-carved Ruthwell Cross made the village famous

Ruthwell's banking museum commemorates the world's first savings bank, set up here in 1810

preacher, writer, editor, antiquarian, enthusiastic curler, philanthropist and pioneering banker.

It was in Ruthwell that he started the world's first savings bank, in a cottage which is now a banking museum.

And it was Dr. Duncan who rescued from disregarded decay one of the finest Dark Age sculptures in Europe, the magnificent 7th-century Ruthwell Cross, with its four faces of intricately carved Biblical scenes. It is now installed in a specially constructed apse in the parish church.

🚗 *RUTHWELL is off the B724, 7 miles west of Annan.*

THORNHILL
Nithsdale

The first village on this site, on a gentle rise of ground above the River Nith, was built in 1664 as the burgh of New Dalgarno. But Thornhill took its place in the late 18th century, built to plans approved by the Duke of Queensberry. It is a very pleasant little town, with a wide main street centred on a Queensberry monument.

In 1810 the Queensberry title was merged with that of Buccleuch, and the present Duke of Buccleuch's Dumfries-shire home is the superb 17th-century Drumlanrig Castle upstream from Thornhill, in wooded parkland near the river. It was built for the 1st Duke of Queensberry, who eccentrically spent only one night in it, then continued to live elsewhere.

On display are the castle's oak panelled state rooms, and very valuable collections of furniture and paintings.

THORNHILL is on the A76, 14 miles north-west of Dumfries.

WANLOCKHEAD
Nithsdale

This is the highest village in Scotland — an old lead-mining settlement almost 1400 ft up in the bleak landscape of the Lowther Hills. Gold used to be panned in the Wanlock Burn, hence the street name Goldscaur Row.

A mining museum in Goldscaur Row has a visitor trail which includes the walk-in Lochnell Mine.

Among the indoor displays is a model of the Leadhills Light Railway, which crossed the highest standard-gauge summit in Britain at 1498 ft between Wanlockhead and Leadhills. Part of the old track-bed, closed in 1938, is being rebuilt as an enthusiast-run narrow gauge line.

WANLOCKHEAD is on the B797, 6 miles north-east of Mennock.

The area around Wanlockhead has been mined since Roman times and the remains of old mine workings can be seen

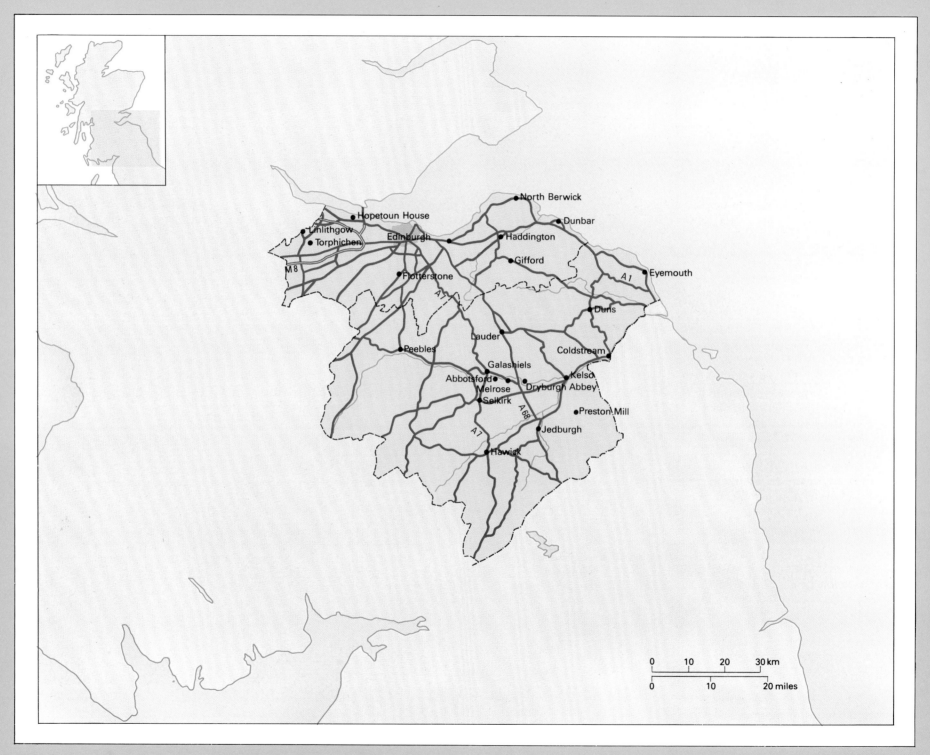

North Berwick

Hopetoun House

Linlithgow
Torphichen
Edinburgh
Haddington
Dunbar

M 8
Gifford
Flotterstone
A 1
Eyemouth

A 7
Duns

Lauder

Peebles
Coldstream

Galashiels
Kelso
Abbotsford
Melrose
Dryburgh Abbey
Selkirk
A 68
Preston Mill

A 7
Jedburgh

Hawick

0   10   20   30 km

0   10   20 miles

Lothian & Borders

The ruins of Dryburgh Abbey, stark against the evening sky, stand on a tongue of land reaching out into the beautiful River Tweed

WHILE EDINBURGH IS the historic capital of Scotland — the Festival City with a Royal palace, a spectacularly located castle, elegant Georgian terraces, allusions to literary personalities at almost every corner — it also has a spreading hinterland.

Stately homes and fishing harbours, inland gardens and a multitude of beautifully conserved estate villages of the 18th and 19th centuries make sure that any visitor is seriously embarrassed for choice.

In the south, Lothian Region rises to a boundary of rounded hill ranges — the Pentlands, the Moorfoots and the Lammermuirs. Beyond them is the Border country, fought over by generations of armies.

Now, this is an area of quiet and reflective river valleys, most of whose waters eventually congregate into the Tweed, sturdily independent towns, mellow ruined abbeys and some prodigious mansions.

One man is the common link here, not simply because of the ballads and novels with which he kept his early 19th-century readers enthralled, and not simply because in his travels as a Sheriff he was well known personally to mighty landlords and poorer folk alike.

In his straightforwardness and honesty, his punishing work schedule and intimate knowledge of his native land, Sir Walter Scott was a man of whom nobody who met him had an ill word to say.

It is a lasting tribute to him that this part of Scotland is still referred to, without affectation, as the Scott Country.

ABBOTSFORD
Ettrick and Lauderdale

Sir Walter Scott had good historic grounds for changing the inelegant name of the farm he bought in 1812 from Cartleyhole to Abbotsford: the house looked over meadows to the Tweed, where the monks of Melrose Abbey once crossed it by a ford.

It was here that — in between relentless spells of writing the best-selling and influential *Waverley* novels — he lived the life of a Border laird; latterly in the present mansion of Abbotsford, which was completed in 1824. And it was here in 1832 that in his last illness he had his bed taken to a riverside room through whose open windows would come the sound of the murmuring waters of the Tweed.

Since then, Abbotsford has always been lived in by his direct descendants. Much of it is open to the public, with his splendid 9000-volume library and remarkable collection of relics of famous and diverse characters like Robert Burns, Flora MacDonald, Rob Roy MacGregor, Napoleon and Charles Edward Stuart.

ABBOTSFORD *is on the B6360, 2 miles west of Melrose.*

COLDSTREAM
Berwickshire

For almost 1000 years, Coldstream has been a major border crossing between Scotland and England, beside a ford replaced in 1776 by John Smeaton's bridge across the Tweed.

The old toll-house on the Scottish side of the bridge was the scene of many a clandestine marriage between English couples, often just ahead of outraged parents racing from the south.

The town gave its name to the

Sir Walter Scott spent many happy years on his estate at Abbotsford

Coldstream Guards, and there is a regimental collection in the museum in the market square. The regiment has the distinction of being the oldest corps in continuous existence in the British Army.

Nearby, a long-dismantled Cistercian priory has left behind little more than the name of Abbey Road, the Nuns' Walk along the bank of the Tweed, and the Penitents' Walk up the side of the tributary River Leet.

Outside Coldstream, the Leet flows through the Hirsel estate of the Douglas-Homes. The estate is open to the public all through the year, with a fine exhibition centre, riverside walks and meandering footpaths through the rhododendron plantations in Dundock Wood.

COLDSTREAM *is on the A698, 9 miles north-east of Kelso.*

DRYBURGH ABBEY
Ettrick and Lauderdale

One of the most beautiful stretches of the River Tweed is at the sweeping double-back bend where, on a tongue of land now laid out with fields and lawns and specimen trees, the ruins of the Premonstratensians' 12th-century Dryburgh Abbey stand.

Dryburgh was farther off the beaten track than the other great Border abbeys, but like them it suffered drastically in the incessant 14th to 16th-century cross-border raids. It was finally left in ruins in 1544.

And yet, a remarkable amount of Dryburgh remains to be looked after as an ancient monument — cloister, transepts, chapter-house and the 15th-century rose window high in the refectory wall.

Sir Walter Scott, who had a family claim to the right of burial here, lies in the north transept. Nearby is the grave of the World War I commander Earl Haig of Bemersyde, the ancestral estate bought back for him by public subscription in 1921.

DRYBURGH *is across the Tweed from St Boswells on the A68.*

DUNBAR
East Lothian

Weather records prove that this is one of the sunniest resorts in Scotland, and it takes full advantage of that, with two 18-hole golf courses, other sports facilities and a fine clifftop trail, part of the John Muir Country Park which extends along eight and a half miles of fascinating coastline towards the dunes, woodlands, rocks

Besides a fine collection of books, Scott's library contains relics of eminent historical figures

and saltmarshes of Belhaven Bay and the estuary of the River Tyne.

John Muir was a powerful advocate of the National Park movement in the United States, and the house in the High Street where he was born in 1838 is now a museum.

Dunbar's fishing fleet is based on the New or Victoria Harbour of 1842, in a splendid situation overlooked by the red-sandstone ruin of Dunbar Castle, now a nesting place for sea birds.

A town trail points out many of the Georgian and earlier buildings at the heart of this dignified old burgh.

DUNBAR is on the A1087, 6 miles east of East Linton.

DUNS
Berwickshire

The site of an ancient hill fort on Duns Law gave this market town and administrative centre its name: here, as in the Highlands and Islands, 'dun' was the Celtic word for just such a fortification.

A footpath to the 714-ft summit, where a Covenanter army gathered in 1639, opens up a wide-spreading view over the rich farmlands of the Merse of Berwickshire to the Cheviot Hills on the southern horizon.

The Jim Clark Room in Newtown Street displays more than 100 trophies won during his career by one of the world's most highly respected Grand Prix drivers.

Manderston, 'the finest Edwardian country house in Britain', is just outside the town. The mansion with its lavish furnishings, extravagantly equipped stables and even a marble dairy is open regularly in the summer. And the Biscuit Tin Museum is a clue to the business on which the family fortunes were founded.

DUNS is on the A6105, 16 miles west of Berwick.

EDINBURGH
City of Edinburgh

Princes Street in Edinburgh may have some ill-advised modern shop frontages, but it remains one of the most impressively located city-centre streets in Europe, dominated by the great basalt cliffs on which Edinburgh Castle stands.

Every year, the castle esplanade is the scene of the Military Tattoo, one of the most atmospheric events of the Edinburgh International Festival, especially when, the sky being dark, a lone piper is spotlighted on a high balcony.

Downhill to the east of the castle, the Royal Mile is extravagantly historic; and at almost every step there are buildings steeped in literary memories — like Lady Stair's House with its displays on Burns, Scott and Stevenson.

The Royal Mile finishes at the Palace of Holyroodhouse, the Queen's official residence in Scotland. Around and above the Palace stretches Holyrood Park, whose name may conjure up gracious Lowland landscaping, but is in fact all sweeping grassy swards, steep footpaths and rugged cliffs leading up to the spectacular viewpoint summit of the old volcano called Arthur's Seat.

The prosperous legal, banking, mercantile, literary and philosophical centre which Edinburgh became in the 18th century far outgrew its original setting around the Royal Mile. One of the most graceful city layouts in the world is the New Town begun in the 1770s — all unselfconsciously elegant Georgian terraces and crescents; and a second New Town was started in the 1820s.

Away from the centre, with its museums, art galleries, concert halls, memorials and formal gardens, Edinburgh is no kind of homogeneous city

(above) **Built on volcanic rock, Edinburgh Castle dominates the city** *(left)* **The magnificent gates to the Palace of Holyroodhouse**

— rather a collection of loosely connected villages.

The old weavers' village of Duddingston has a bird sanctuary round its loch, and the oldest pub in Scotland.

Dean Village is an astonishingly carefully restored place, established in the 12th century by millers and bakers and tanners, but now almost entirely residential in its half-secret location by the Water of Leith.

And Cramond, with its narrow anchorage at the mouth of the River Almond, where the white-walled, red-roofed houses were once the home of oyster fishermen, has been settled since Roman times. It was a port for the materials that went into the building of Antonine's Wall, the northern frontier of the Roman Empire. Roman ships based here were the first to sail right round Britain.

🚗 *EDINBURGH is 45 miles east of Glasgow.*

EYEMOUTH
Berwickshire

There have been North Sea fishermen based on this historic little town since the 12th century. Trawlers and shellfish boats still operate from John Smeaton's shrewdly designed harbour of 1768, at the rocky mouth of the Eye Water.

In 1597, Eyemouth was declared a free port. This led to one unexpected development: especially in the 18th century, it became a highly organised smuggling centre. Gunsgreen House, still overlooking the river from the east bank, was built with secret storage chambers and underground passages all around it.

After the smuggling days, Eyemouth men went back full-time to fishing, and this was the scene of the greatest fishing-fleet disaster in Scottish waters: on 14 October 1881, no fewer than 23 boats and 129 fishermen were lost in a furious storm.

Near the quay where catches are auctioned, the Eyemouth Museum has extensive displays on the place itself, its fishing and the marine wildlife of the coast; and there is an almost million-stitch tapestry.

🚗 *EYEMOUTH is on the B6355, 8 miles north of Berwick.*

FLOTTERSTONE
Midlothian

The Pentland Hills rise directly from the south-western suburbs of Edinburgh, extending for miles, with many individual grassy summits, gentle passes, quiet valleys and a network of pathways.

One of the main access points is at Flotterstone, the start of a tarmac road which can be used by walkers as it curls into a Highland-looking glen to service the reservoirs at Glencorse and Loganlea.

The hill immediately west of Flotterstone was the scene in 1666 of the Battle of Rullion Green, in which government troops — after a first rebuff — heavily defeated an outnumbered force of Covenanters.

This was the subject of Robert Louis Stevenson's first-ever published work. His booklet called *The Pentland Rising* was dated exactly 200 years after the event.

🚗 *FLOTTERSTONE is on the A702, 4 miles south of Fairmilehead.*

GALASHIELS
Ettrick and Lauderdale

This substantial town with an often abbreviated name, at the foot of the valley of the Gala Water just before it flows into the Tweed, grew up as a textile centre. It was the Gala weavers who, by forming themselves into a trade corporation, created the basis of a textile *industry*, where only small, individual producers had existed before.

That was in 1777. Textiles in Galashiels reached their peak in late-Victorian times, when the names of almost 30 mills and dyeworks were recorded. Their numbers have been drastically reduced, and Galashiels has been forced to diversify. But its Nether Mill is still the largest producer of woollen tartan cloth in the world, with more than 700 patterns in stock.

Nether Mill also has an exhibition on the woollen industry, which merges into another one on the history of the town.

The war memorial in Galashiels picks up that theme. It includes a fine statue, by a local sculptor, of an armed, mounted and ready-for-action Border reiver.

🚗 *GALASHIELS is on the A7, 3 miles west of Melrose.*

GIFFORD
East Lothian

Three villages along the northern fringe of the Lammermuir Hills are among the architectural showpieces of East Lothian. Gifford is the biggest of them, dating from the 17th century but laid out to a largely Georgian and Victorian plan.

The remarkable tapestry of almost a million stitches in the Eyemouth Museum, sited near the quay

The architect of its parish church, built in 1710, obviously had Dutch as well as Scottish designs in mind; and a memorial here recalls that the Reverend John Witherspoon, who signed the American Declaration of Independence, was a son of the Gifford manse.

A reconstructed market cross and the elegant town house with its Victorian clock tower face an avenue of limes which leads to the ornamental gates of Yester House.

A few miles to the north-east, Garvald is an attractively tucked away tangle of red-stone and pantile-roofed cottages in the valley of the Papana Water. Above it is the modern Cistercian Abbey of Nunraw.

Stenton is a beautifully preserved 18th and early 19th-century village, with an earlier dovecot tower and the re-erected scales on which bartered goods were weighed.

In 1819 a hill burn south of Stenton was dammed to create the narrow and winding mile-long Pressmennan Lake, where a Forestry Commission trail now runs through shady plantations of spruce, oak and larch.

GIFFORD *is on the B6355, 11 miles south-west of Dunbar.*

Common Ridings

One thing more than any other which shows the local spirit of the Border towns is the Common Ridings — that tradition of riding round the town's boundaries to check that there had been no encroachments on its common land.

Every festival has its leading personalities — the Melrosian and the Festival Queen at Melrose; the Cornet and his Lass at Peebles, Hawick and Lauder; the Braw Lad and the Braw Lass at Galashiels; the Reiver and his Lass at Duns.

Early on the Friday of Selkirk Common Riding almost the whole town joins in procession to sing *Hail, Smiling Morn*; one of Jedburgh's songs echoes the town's old authentic battle-cry *Jethart's Here!*

Not all the battles and skirmishes recalled in the ceremonies were Scottish victories. James IV's disastrous defeat in 1513 at Flodden in Northumberland still stirs the emotions.

In Coldstream Civic Week there is a ride-out across the border so that the Coldstreamer can lay a wreath on the Flodden memorial.

And Selkirk Common Riding has one heart-stopping moment: the Standard Bearer, re-enacting the traditional way in which the sole survivor of the 80 Selkirk men who went to fight at Flodden — too struck down by emotion to speak — brought back the news of the overwhelming defeat, 'casts the colours' in the market place. Other standards are then cast down to honour the dead of later wars.

But these festivals are, above all, exuberant celebrations.

They feature parades and processions, firework displays, music and dancing, sports and even — at Kelso — a raft race down the Tweed.

The annual raft race down the Tweed begins at Kelso where a fine bridge by John Rennie spans the river

HADDINGTON
East Lothian

Very few places in Scotland are as wholeheartedly devoted to architectural conservation as Haddington, the business and administrative centre of East Lothian, and once the county town of what was originally called Haddingtonshire.

This explains the presence of elegant town mansions built for county families, the banks and public buildings.

The early 17th-century Haddington House is the headquarters of the enthusiastic trust which co-ordinates many of the town's projects. Its wall-ed garden is laid out in contemporary Scottish style, featuring a laburnum walk and sunken flower beds.

Within strolling distance are the largely restored, basically 14th-century St Mary's Church; an 18th-century dovecot which houses an exhibition on the history of the town; and an elegant red-sandstone footbridge over the gentle River Tyne to the new but appropriately designed houses in the ancient suburb of Nungate.

There is a museum in the Georgian heart of the town devoted to the writer Thomas Carlyle and his locally-born wife Jane Welsh. And among the colour-washed house fron-tages there are many intriguing smaller details — like the recurring motif of a goat. Haddington's coat of arms has the puzzling combination of a goat with a bunch of grapes.

HADDINGTON *is off the A1, 10 miles west of Dunbar.*

HAWICK
Roxburgh

Largest of the Border towns, Hawick is centred on a narrow but busy High Street in which the oldest building is the Tower Hotel, once the town house of the Douglas and then the Scott families, but converted into a coaching inn during the 1770s.

Among its notable guests have been William and Dorothy Wordsworth, whom Sir Walter Scott brought here in 1803 when he was escorting them on part of a Border tour.

Hawick has three main preoccupations: its busy woollen industry which sends cashmere, Shetland and lambswool knitwear, as well as tweeds and tartans, all over the world; sales of livestock from the well-farmed valleys and upland grazings nearby; and — like the Border towns — an almost overwhelming interest in rugby.

The town is built along both banks of the Teviot, and features a 107-acre riverside park around the mansion-house of Wilton Lodge.

Here, there are walled gardens and walks, a local-history museum and the re-erected market cross, and a memorial to one of Hawick's most famous sportsmen, the international motorcycle racer Jimmy Guthrie — killed in 1937 in an accident while competing, like Jim Clark a generation later, in an event in Germany.

HAWICK *is on the A7, 23 miles north of Langholm.*

HOPETOUN HOUSE
West Lothian

Although it looks like a single part of a grand architectural and landscape plan, this majestic mansion house in wooded parkland above the Firth of Forth — home of the Marquess of Linlithgow — is actually one house grafted onto another.

Between 1599 and 1603 Sir William Bruce was the architect of what is now the central part of the house. William Adam began adding to the masterly work with substantial wings on either side; he was still engaged on it at the time of his death in 1748, and the interior decoration was finished by his sons Robert and John — 19

Court Street in the former county town of Haddington is a tribute to sensitive architectural conservation

years later.

Hopetoun has lavishly furnished state rooms with beautiful Adam plasterwork, wood-carvings, tapestries and portraits.

In the north-wing pavilion there is an exhibition on 'Horse and Man in Lowland Scotland'. And the tour of the main house includes a visit to the Roof Observatory, which is actually a high-level viewpoint over the estate woodlands to the two Forth Bridges.

A very attractive nature trail looks down from yew hedges to a red deer park bounded on the north by the estuary of the Forth, and finishes along a lime avenue back towards the grand old house.

HOPETOUN HOUSE *is reached from South Queensferry, off the A90 north-west of Edinburgh.*

JEDBURGH
Roxburgh

Since it is on one of the main cross-border roads, this historic town with a finely restored centre has been visited by many famous travellers: Bonnie Prince Charlie in 1745; Robert Burns in 1787, when he was made a freeman of the burgh and charmed its ladies; and Sir Walter Scott, who made his first courtroom appearance as a lawyer here in 1793.

But the visitor who made the greatest impression was Mary, Queen of Scots. She spent some time in 1566 living in a fortified mansion-house which is now a notably well-furnished museum among gardens overlooking the Jed Water.

Jedburgh's splendid ruined abbey was founded in 1118. Like the other great religious houses in the Borders, it never recovered from the notorious 'Rough Wooing' of the 1540s.

This was the invasion whose unsuccessful purpose was to force the Scots to allow the infant Queen Mary to be betrothed to Henry VIII's son and heir, thus eventually uniting both kingdoms under a Tudor monarch.

Instead, in 1603, they were united under Mary's son James, when the succession fell to the Stuarts.

In the higher part of the town, Jedburgh Castle is misleadingly named. The original castle changed hands so many times in the border wars that in 1409 the Scots exasperatedly demolished it.

The present building — now a comprehensive but highly unusual museum — may have battlemented curtain walls, a dummy portcullis and ornamental towers; but it was built in the 1820s to serve as a prison.

JEDBURGH *is on the A68, 12 miles north of the border at Carter Bar.*

KELSO
Roxburgh

This is another Border town which grew up beside a 12th-century abbey. Kelso Abbey, on a curve of the Tweed just after it is joined by the Teviot, was the most substantial religious house in the Borders; but it was another victim of the Rough Wooing, and what the English left standing was further reduced at the time of the Reformation in 1560.

Kelso's central square is one of the great Georgian townscapes of the Borders. Livestock sales used to be held there, but they have moved across John Rennie's five-arched bridge of 1803 to Springwood Park on the far bank of the Tweed, which is also the site of the famous Border Union agricultural show.

There is a racecourse outside the town. The Tweed and, to a lesser extent, the Teviot are well-known salmon rivers. Rugby is the favourite game, but Kelso cricket club has been in operation since 1821.

The priory at Jedburgh was founded for the Augustinian Canons in 1118 and made an abbey in 1147

A short distance up-river from Kelso, the Tweed curves past the parkland of Floors Castle, home of the Duke of Roxburghe. William Adam's original restrained Georgian mansion was almost swamped by the unbridled ornamentation — and massive new wings — added by William Playfair in Victorian times.

This is the largest inhabited house in Scotland, with a window for every day in the year. Guided tours show off some of the rooms and their fine collection of portraits. The gardens are open at the same times as the castle, and the grounds are a favourite venue for horse-driving trials.

 KELSO is on the A698, 10 miles north-east of Jedburgh.

LAUDER
Ettrick and Lauderdale

This ancient burgh at the heart of Lauderdale has been involved in many historic events. In 1483, for instance, James III's courtiers, exasperated by the King's reliance on low-born advisers, insisted that six of them be hanged from the old Lauder bridge.

Lauder Tolbooth on its island site is a constantly rebuilt version of the 1318 original. The parish church of 1673 is a curious design, to a Greek-cross plan, surmounted by an octagonal steeple.

The Southern Upland Way crosses the main road here and passes through the grounds of Thirlestane Castle, built for Mary, Queen of Scots' private secretary Maitland of Lethington and extended in Restoration style for his descendant the 1st Duke of Lauderdale.

After massive renovations, the castle, whose decorated plasterwork ceilings have few equals in Europe, is open to the public. Part of it is now the Border Country Life Museum.

 LAUDER is on the A68, 27 miles south-east of Edinburgh.

LINLITHGOW
West Lothian

Motorists on the M9 have one of the most striking views of the old county town of West Lothian, where a royal palace of the Stuarts looks down over lawns to Linlithgow Loch, and behind it stands the imposing, mostly 15th-century St Michael's parish church with its modern sculptured spire.

Edward I of England fortified this site as his headquarters during the winter campaign of 1301/2. But work on the present palace started in 1425, during the reign of James I.

Many other Stuart personalities were closely involved with Linlithgow. James V and his daughter Mary, Queen of Scots were born here; Charles I spent a single night in the palace; and Bonnie Prince Charlie passed through during the last Jacobite Rising which tried to put the Stuarts back on the throne.

Ironically, much of the building was destroyed in a fire started while the Duke of Cumberland's troops were in occupation in 1746. Now it is partly restored, and is a very impressive ancient monument.

Thanks to its royal connections and its status as the county town, Linlithgow has a fine centre, with many 17th to 19th-century buildings in the East and West High Streets.

North-east of the town is the House of the Binns, home of the Dalyells and now owned by the National Trust for Scotland. It contains many relics of Sir Thomas Dalyell, Charles II's commander-in-chief in the ferocious campaign against the Covenanters.

In the hills to the south of Linlithgow, Beecraigs County Park includes more than 700 acres of

Linlithgow Palace, the ruined birthplace of Mary, Queen of Scots

woodlands crossed by footpaths and bridleways, a good visitor centre and a trout lake formed from a redundant reservoir.

🚗 *LINLITHGOW is off the M9, 17 miles west of Edinburgh.*

MELROSE
Ettrick and Lauderdale

High above the beautifully placed Tweed-side town of Melrose are the three rounded summits of the Eildon Hills. Eildon Hill North was settled, 2000 years ago, by a tribe known to the Romans as the Selgovae, whose vast circular earthwork, enclosing the sites of nearly 300 turf houses, can still be traced round the summit today.

The Romans took over the same hilltop for a signal station, watching over the road to their major settlement of Trimontium — 'the three mountains'. Much later, as Newstead, this was the home of the masons who built Melrose Abbey, which was established by Cistercian monks in the 1140s.

Robert the Bruce's heart is believed to be buried in the Abbey; he was one of several kings who endowed the religious house with extensive lands and possessions.

Now, its power and influence long since gone, it stands in stately ruins as a very fine ancient monument.

Next to it, in the National Trust for Scotland's Priorwood Gardens, old strains of apples which the monk-gardeners and even the Romans knew have been re-established, and flowers are prepared for autumn drying.

Melrose is a great rugby town, and it was at the local club's Greenyards ground in 1883 that the seven-a-side game was first played.

The Southern Upland Way crosses the Tweed by Melrose's suspension footbridge of 1826. And the Eildon

Walk heads steeply up towards the hilltop where families of the Selgovae, then watchful Roman legionaries, looked out.

🚗 *MELROSE is 3 miles north-west of Newton St Boswells on the A68.*

NORTH BERWICK
East Lothian

On the outer limit of the Firth of Forth, this holiday resort has long sandy beaches, a yachting harbour and two golf courses on splendid links that stretch to east and west.

Rising immediately to the south is the outstanding viewpoint of North Berwick Law.

Even more spectacular, out in the mouth of the Firth, is the massive, mile-round Bass Rock. Boat trips are run from North Berwick to this towering, cliff-bound outcrop where a lighthouse stands on a terrace below the slanting upper grasslands. Thousands of gannets, gulls and kittiwakes wheel around.

The 7th-century St Baldred is believed to have had his hermit's cell here, and there is a ruined chapel dedicated to him.

In the 1690s, four resourceful men held the island fortress — by that time a state prison — in the Jacobite interest for longer than any other place in Britain.

East of North Berwick, Tantallon Castle is a ruined clifftop stronghold forming an impressive foreground to a view of the Bass.

West of the town there is a coastal nature trail among the woods and sea-buckthorn of Yellowcraig.

🚗 *NORTH BERWICK is on the A198, 12 miles north-west of Dunbar.*

Despite the depradations of the English, Melrose Abbey retains some fine decorative work and sculpture

The former county town of Peebles, with Mercat Cross — a 12ft high octagonal column dating back to 1320 — in the foreground

PEEBLES
Tweeddale

Forest trails on the hills of Glentress to the east, a golf course on the open hillside to the west, parks and riverside walks along the River Tweed which runs through the town, rounded hills and valleys stretching away to the south — all these features combine to give Peebles a setting of great variety and charm.

It is an old-established county town, a royal burgh after the granting of a charter by David I in the 12th century.

Dignified frontages of 17th to 19th-century buildings line the lively High Street; and tucked away in Cross Road is the protected ruin of the Cross Kirk of 1261.

Peebles is within easy reach of several notable buildings open to the public, up and down Tweeddale.

West of the town, poised dramatically above a narrow and wooded stretch of the river, Neidpath Castle is a fortified 14th-century tower remodelled as more of a family home 300 years later.

Farther up-river, the parish church of Stobo is in authentic Norman style. Nearby, the extensively wooded Dawyck estate is an out-station of the Royal Botanic Garden in Edinburgh.

Downstream from Peebles, Traquair House dates in part from 1107 and is said to be the oldest inhabited house in Scotland. It has many mementoes of the Stuart kings to whom its lairds were related, and of the tragic Mary, Queen of Scots who stayed here with Darnley in 1566.

Traquair is famous for its Bear Gates, which are not to be opened until another Stuart takes the throne.

In an altogether different context, it is also known for Traquair Ale, still produced in small quantities in the estate's own 18th-century brewhouse.
PEEBLES is at the junction of the A72 and the A703, 23 miles south of Edinburgh.

PRESTON MILL
East Lothian

One of the smallest properties of the National Trust for Scotland — but also one of the most attractive in its fabric, its immediate surroundings and the authenticity of its restoration — is this sole-surviving example of the meal-mills of the lower River Tyne.

Preston Mill dates mainly from the 17th century, although there have been millers here for something like 800 years.

With its seemingly random outbuildings, the grain-drying kiln with its wind-directional vane, and all the

Millers have worked in the idyllic setting of Preston Mill, the last mill on the lower River Tyne, for about 800 years

roofs covered in East Lothian's favourite red pantiles, Preston Mill is a photographers' and artists' delight.
🚗 *PRESTON MILL is on the B1407, north-east of East Linton.*

SELKIRK
Ettrick and Lauderdale

Higher set than the other Border towns, Selkirk is on a hillside above the textile mills along the Ettrick Water. It was often the base of the Scottish kings, on their way to the royal hunting reserve of Ettrick Forest.

In the upper part of the town is the Market Place, with its statue of Sir Walter Scott. He was here many times in real life — as one of the Sheriffs of Selkirkshire — hearing cases in the now-disappeared Tolbooth on whose site his statue stands, and after 1803 in the Court-room beside it, where mementoes of him are retained.

On the west side of the square, Halliwell's Close leads to a restored 18th-century house which is partly a local-history museum and partly a museum of vintage ironmongery.

Farther up the Ettrick Water, among fields and sweeping woodlands, Bowhill House is the mostly 19th-century Border home of the Duke of Buccleuch. It is open in summer to show its grandly furnished state rooms and valuable collection of paintings.

Two attractive and informative woodland trails meander through the grounds, past ornamental lochs and along the banks of the Ettrick's major tributary, the Yarrow Water.
🚗 *SELKIRK is on the A7, 7 miles south of Galashiels.*

TORPHICHEN
West Lothian

The Knights of the medieval Order of St John chose this location for the preceptory which became their Scottish headquarters — and the heart of a sanctuary area. Its central tower and transepts remain as an ancient monument, and the rebuilt nave is a parish church.

On the summit of Cairnpapple Hill, south-east of the village, there is a remarkable ceremonial and burial site, first used around 4000 years ago. A dome now protects the excavated site, and allows some of the early graves to be displayed.

One element in Cairnpapple's mystic appeal must have been that, in clear conditions, the view extends all the way across Central Scotland, literally from sea to sea.
🚗 *TORPHICHEN is on the B792, 2 miles north of Bathgate.*

85

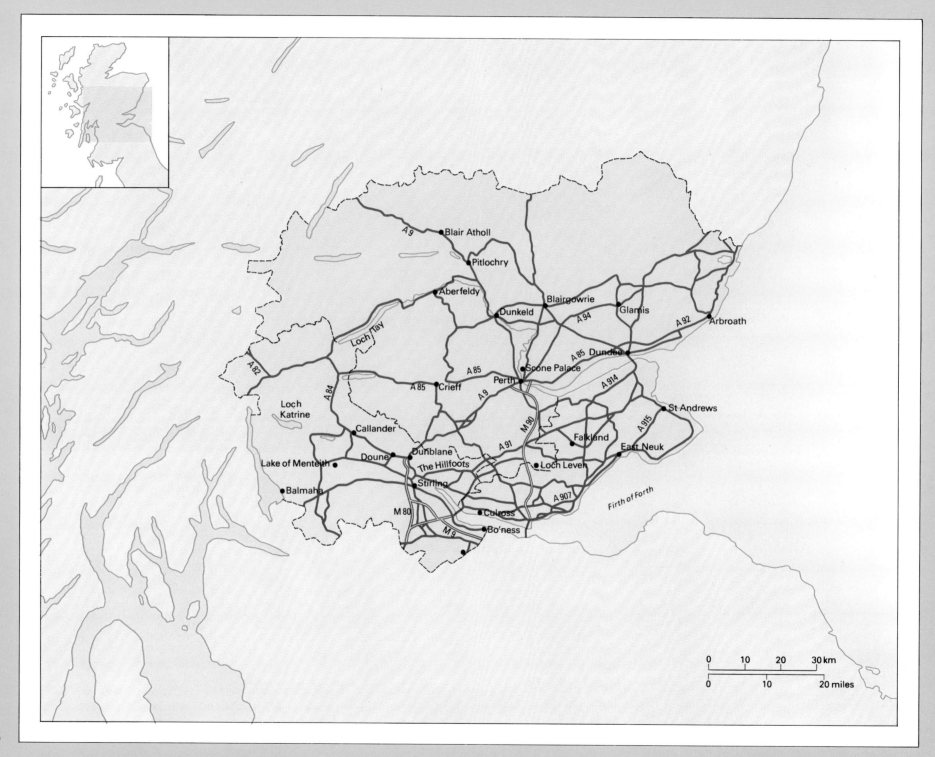

Blair Atholl

Pitlochry

Aberfeldy

A 9

Loch Tay

A 82

A 84

Loch Katrine

Callander

Lake of Menteith

Balmaha

Doune

Dunblane

The Hillfoots

Stirling

M 80

M 9

Culross

Bo'ness

Dunkeld

Blairgowrie

Glamis

A 94

A 92

Arbroath

A 85

Dundee

Scone Palace

Perth

A 85

Crieff

A 9

A 91

A 90

A 914

St Andrews

A 315

Falkland

East Neuk

Loch Leven

A 907

Firth of Forth

0   10   20   30 km

0   10   20 miles

Central, Fife & Tayside

Walter Scott's ballad *The Lady of the Lake* was inspired by Loch Katrine, a fact which draws many visitors. Summer cruises can be taken on a turn-of-the-century steamer named after the great man

*I*F THERE WERE A prize for the most boring name handed out to any of Scotland's new Regions in the local government reorganisation of 1975, it would have to go to Central. The name conjures up visions of ...... nothing very alluring.

And yet, this is the area which includes places like the Trossachs — the lochsides, mountains and forests where Sir Walter Scott set many of his romances, and Rob Roy MacGregor was a real-life outlaw; almost the whole of the eastern side of Loch Lomond, with its oakwoods and offshore islands; historic cathedrals, monuments, battlefields, full-scale mountains and miles of hill and forest walks.

In that same reshuffle of boundaries and names, the old 'Kingdom' of

Fife fought an impressive battle to remain separate and complete.

This massive peninsula between the estuaries of the Forth and the Tay is far from being — in a King of Scotland's one-time jibe — 'a beggar's mantle with a fringe of gold'. The fringe is certainly still there, in the string of beautifully restored little coastal towns and sandy beaches; but the interior of Fife has its own fair share of the spirit of conserving the attractive and historic fabric of the past.

Tayside is mostly the former counties of Perth, Angus and Kinross. The miles upon miles of arable farms in Strathmore and the Carse of Gowrie, separated by the rounded Sidlaw Hills, are balanced by coastal towns, cliffs and inland mountain glens.

ABERFELDY
Perth and Kinross

Coming here in 1787, Robert Burns was delighted by a walk through the wooded ravine around the Moness Falls on the outskirts of the town, and wrote the still-popular song called *The Birks of Aberfeldy*.

The birks (or birches) and many other trees still flourish, and the glen now has a beautiful nature trail.

Aberfeldy lies in the valley of the River Tay, with sweeping hills to north and south. Beside General Wade's bridge of 1733 is the Black Watch memorial; the famous regiment was raised here in 1739, and its original duty was to keep watch on the Jacobite clans.

To the north-west of Aberfeldy, the sturdy 16th-century Castle Menzies is being restored by the Clan Menzies Society. On either side of the town are the colourful shrub and woodland gardens at Bolfracks and Cluny House. And, off the Grantully road, the 16th-century St Mary's church is preserved as an ancient monument because of its intricately painted ceiling.

🚗 *ABERFELDY is on the A827, 23 miles north of Crieff.*

ARBROATH
Angus

The most significant building in this independent-minded fishing town is the ruined 12th-century Abbey, where the Declaration of Arbroath was composed in 1320.

Six years after Bruce's victory at Bannockburn had reasserted Scotland's independence, there were still innumerable nuisances and border raids. The Declaration, written in clerical Latin, was addressed to Pope John XXII in an effort to have him convince the English that the war

was over. Even then, the formal peace treaty was not signed until 1328.

Nowadays, the town's most famous product is the 'Arbroath smokie'. Haddock bought at the quayside fish market are put into curing sheds, and then sold all over Scotland.

There is a breezy clifftop nature trail to the north-east; and a comprehensive local museum is contained in a notable building — the early 19th-century Signal Tower from which communication was maintained in pre-radio times with Bell Rock Lighthouse 11 miles out to sea.

🚗 *ARBROATH is on the A92, 16 miles north-east of Dundee.*

BALMAHA
Stirling

This gorgeously situated Loch Lomondside village, with its

Arbroath smokies, a popular national dish

boatyard, yacht and dinghy moorings, is sheltered from the north by the descending summits of Conic Hill. They mark the edge of the Highland Boundary Fault.

Inchcailloch, the island immediately opposite Balmaha, has a beautiful Nature Conservancy trail through hilly oak and alder woodlands — browsed by fallow deer — which were once commercially cropped. There is also the site of a 13th-century church and burial ground.

On the mainland, pathways climb through larch and spruce plantations to glorious viewpoints on Conic Hill, down which the West Highland Way approaches Balmaha before continuing up the lochside to Rowardennan at the foot of Ben Lomond.

Balmaha is also the starting point for the regular passenger-carrying island mailboat run.

🚗 *BALMAHA is on the B837, 3½ miles west of Drymen.*

BLAIR ATHOLL
Perth and Kinross

This is the village at the gates of Blair Castle, the dignified white-towered home, surrounded by wooded parkland, of the Duke of Atholl. The oldest part of the castle dates from 1270, and no fewer than 32 of its apartments are open to visitors, from supremely elegant state rooms to the passageway called the Fourth Duke's Corridor.

The Duke of Atholl is the only person in Europe to be allowed a private army — a privilege granted by Queen Victoria. One of the great events at Blair Castle is the Atholl Highlanders' annual inspection and parade.

Blair Atholl has a local museum and a working old-style corn mill.

Three miles west, the Clan Donnachaidh Museum is devoted to the families of Robertson, Reid and Duncan. It is at the foot of the steeply wooded glen where paths and footbridges show off the triple cascades of the Falls of Bruar.

🚗 *BLAIR ATHOLL is off the A9, 7 miles north of Pitlochry.*

BLAIRGOWRIE
Perth and Kinross

On opposite banks of the rushing River Ericht, Blairgowrie and Rattray combine to form a single town which, thanks to the hundreds of acres of soft-fruit farms around it, is no less than 'raspberry capital of the world'.

The soft-fruit industry started in the 1890s. Before that, the waters of the Ericht powered a series of now-abandoned flax and jute mills.

One point on the river is still known as Cargill's Leap, after a hair-raising escape from pursuing soldiers by one of the most famous of all the Covenanting preachers, the Rattray-born Reverend Donald Cargill.

Blair Castle is the 13th-century stronghold of the Duke of Atholl. Within its handsome walls are displays of china, weaponry and Jacobite relics

South of the town, the suburb of Rosemount is the home of Blairgowrie Golf Club, whose courses set among heather banks, pines and birchwoods are among the finest inland layouts in Scotland.

To the west, Ardblair Castle, home of the Blair-Oliphant family descended from Bonnie Prince Charlie's aide-de-camp, is open on certain days to display its Jacobite relics.

🚗 *BLAIRGOWRIE is on the A93, 16 miles north of Perth.*

BO'NESS
Falkirk

Built on rising ground on the south side of the Firth of Forth, this once heavily industrialised town has long since given up its fuller name of Borrowstounness; the old shipyards, whaling dock, salt-pans, coal-mines and potteries have also gone, along with a flourishing trade in pit-props imported from the Baltic.

Handsomely situated above the town, and noted for its ornamented walls and ceilings, the old mansion-house of Kinneil — once a seat of the Dukes of Hamilton — is preserved in an attractive public park with fine views across the Forth to the hills of Fife.

A Roman fort built as part of the Antonine Wall has been uncovered in the Kinneil grounds, and the old stables block has been turned into an excellent local-history museum.

On the shore of the Forth, the volunteer-run Bo'ness and Kinneil Railway offers steam-hauled services on summer weekends.

🚗 *BO'NESS is on the A706, 3 miles north of Linlithgow.*

CALLANDER
Stirling

There are traces of a remoter past in and around Callander — a Roman fort, and the grassy mound by the meadows of the River Teith named

Culross Palace was the first property bought by the National Trust for Scotland

after the 6th-century St Kessog; but the centre of this attractively laid-out town still follows a plan devised in 1739.

Ancaster Square remains the heart of the plan, with many original houses. A great deal of Callander, though, is 19th-century, built to cater for tourists come to thrill at the district where Sir Walter Scott set so many of his exciting ballads and novels.

Callander has a genuinely Highland backdrop. Behind it rise steep wooded crags which, despite their forbidding appearance, have well-marked footpaths to dramatic summit viewpoints.

There are beautiful autumn beechwoods on the edge of the golf course. High above is another footpath, with spreading views over the Teith valley, to the rock-ledged Bracklinn Falls.

North-west of the town, the main road enters the Highlands proper at the narrow and thickly wooded Pass of Leny, where footpaths follow old charcoal-burners' routes and skirt a deserted village, and there is a famous salmon-leap.

CALLANDER *is on the A84, 16 miles north-west of Stirling.*

CRIEFF
Perth and Kinross

This is another place where Lowlands and Highlands meet — a process which has not always been peaceful. In 1716 the Jacobite army left the town a smoking ruin. Bonnie Prince Charlie, exactly 30 years later, held a war council here during his retreat to Culloden.

But there was normal commercial traffic too: Highland drovers used to bring thousands of cattle to Crieff market.

In mid-Victorian times, the town began to develop as a health and holiday resort. Now it has golf courses, parks, riverside paths like Lady Mary's Walk alongside the Earn, and footpaths climbing the hill called the Knock, where pinewoods, birch and rowan give way to heather moors with magnificent high-level views.

There are artists and craftsmen here too. Crieff produces glassware and pottery, crystal and paperweights on a considerable scale; and the oldest malt whisky distillery in Scotland operates from a quiet nearby glen.

CRIEFF is on the A85, 17 miles west of Perth.

CULROSS
Dunfermline

At the foot of a hill rising from the north shore of the Firth of Forth, Coo'ross is a place in an apparent time-warp. There are no television aerials or telephone poles, and many of its houses are intricate restorations of carelessly attractive 17th-century originals.

Culross once had famous coal mines under the sea, dozens of salt-pans on the shore, blacksmiths' shops and a harbour busy with Dutch and Baltic trade.

Back as ships' ballast from the Netherlands came loads of red-clay pantiles. Together with white-harled walls, outside stairways, crow-stepped gables, dormer windows, turrets and corbels, these have become the architectural mark of the little town.

Most notable of the buildings open to the public — one of several owned by the National Trust for Scotland — is Culross Palace, completed in 1611 for the wealthy merchant laird Sir George Bruce.

A Culross Trail explores all levels of the place, from the Georgian town house, up narrow lanes towards the high-set parish church built alongside the substantial ruin of a 13th-century Cistercian Abbey.

CULROSS is off the A985, 7 miles west of Dunfermline.

Dunblane has picturesque stone-built houses and an ancient cathedral

DOUNE
Stirling

One of Scotland's finest medieval castles stands above the winding and wooded banks of the River Teith on the outskirts of this little town once famous for the manufacture of the pistols which still appear on its coat of arms.

Doune Castle was built around 1380 as the stronghold of the Stuart Duke of Albany, taken over as a residence of the Stuart kings and queens, then given back to the original family, who became the Stuart Earls of Moray. The 20th Earl is the laird of Doune today.

The whole fabric of the castle was restored in the 1880s. Most of it is unfurnished, but rooms shown to visitors include the royal apartments and the dignified Lord's Hall with its heraldic screen displaying 20 coats of arms.

On the far side of the town, Doune Motor Museum is housed in rebuilt 19th-century farm buildings. It has the Earl's own collection as its base.

DOUNE is on the A84, 8 miles north-west of Stirling.

DUNBLANE
Stirling

Although a town in size, Dunblane is sometimes given the courtesy of being called a city, because of the cathedral which was built here beside the Allan Water early in the 12th century — on the site of a Celtic church established by St Blane himself about the year 600.

Carefully-restored buildings at the Cross which forms the heart of the town focus attention on the cathedral.

This is still the parish church, with much of the early stonework restored

Scotland's fourth largest city, Dundee's industrial sprawl covers the north bank of the Firth of Tay

at the turn of the century. The oldest surviving features of the building are a Norman tower and the marble-floored, oak-panelled Lady Chapel.

Buried in the choir are Margaret Drummond, mistress of James IV, and her two sisters. Political intrigue led to their being poisoned at a meal in 1502, to make sure that Margaret would never marry the King.

Now almost entirely surrounded by Dunblane, the little hamlet of Ramoyle, near the cathedral, was visited in Victorian times because of its mineral wells.

South of Dunblane, passing at first below the hillside golf course, the wooded and very attractive Darn Walk follows the river to Bridge of Allan, a town which developed more wholeheartedly as a spa.

DUNBLANE *is on the A9, 5 miles north of Stirling.*

92

DUNDEE
City of Dundee

This is an uncompromisingly industrial city on the north bank of the Firth of Tay, producing — as the local saying has it — 'jute, jam and journalists' in great quantities.

There are many modern factories on the outskirts, whereas in previous centuries the emphasis was on the woollen and linen trade, the docks and the whaling fleet.

From Edward I in 1296 to Cromwell's General Monck in 1651, Dundee attracted a disastrous number of besieging armies and fleets. Very few historic buildings survive, although the Old Steeple of the 15th-century parish church is one of the city's many museums, and the very well restored Claypotts Castle of a century later stands casually among

lawns and gardens at the side of a suburban road.

Dundee has an unexpectedly fine variety of public parks. Camperdown Park houses a golf museum; the Mills Observatory was built in 1935 in Balgay Park, specifically for public use; and the highest park is around Dundee Law, the 571-ft spectacular viewpoint summit of an old volcano.

Down in the harbour is the oldest British warship still afloat: the frigate *Unicorn* launched at Chatham in 1824 and now most impressively equipped as a privately-run naval museum.

DUNDEE *is 21 miles north east of Perth.*

DUNKELD
Perth and Kinross

The town and cathedral here — on a site where a monastery was establish-

ed in the 6th century and some masonry of its 848 replacement can still be seen — both suffered because of their all too accessible position on the main route into the Central Highlands.

In 1560 the Reformers badly damaged the cathedral, which had taken from 1318 to 1501 to reach completion; and in 1689 only three houses in the whole town survived the Battle of Dunkeld, a Pyrrhic victory by a Covenanting regiment over the Jacobites.

Several restorations in more recent years have preserved the remains of the cathedral, on its very pleasant site among wooded lawns above the River Tay. The National Trust for Scotland has painstakingly rebuilt the houses leading up to it — 17th and 18th-century replacements for the town burned down in the battle.

The Tay here is a famous salmon river overlooked by steeply wooded hills. Thomas Telford's seven-arched bridge of 1808 crosses it to the Victorian village of Birnam, where what is claimed to be the last surviving oak of the Birnam Wood in Shakespeare's *Macbeth* is propped up beside the beautiful riverside Terrace Walk.

🚗 *DUNKELD is off the A9, 15 miles north of Perth.*

EAST NEUK
North-east Fife

The string of very attractive little harbour towns and holiday resorts along the coast from Largo Bay to Fife Ness occupy the district known unofficially as the East Neuk — or corner — of Fife.

Earlsferry takes its name from a traditional ferry-crossing over the Forth to the Lothian shore. A curving sandy bay links it with Elie, where the Lady's Tower above the low cliffs beyond the yachting harbour was where the imperious Lady Janet Anstruther used to bathe after sending a bellman round the town to warn the 18th-century commoners away.

St Monance has a handsomely restored 14th-century church, and a yard where fishing boats have been built for well over 200 years.

Along the High Street of Pittenweem there is a fine display of 16th to 18th-century architecture, notably in the 1588 Tolbooth and the stone-towered Kellie Lodging built two years later.

Narrow wynds lead down to the harbour, where the central fish-market of the East Neuk is overlooked by more elegant buildings restored, like so much hereabouts, by the National Trust for Scotland.

Last of the historic East Neuk burghs is Crail. A heritage trail takes

The Birthplace of Golf

Nobody knows for certain when or where golf was first played in Scotland; but there were several 15th-century Acts of Parliament by which the authorities tried — with no great success — to have men of fighting age stop spending time on golf which would have been better devoted to archery practice in preparation for yet another war with the English.

These prohibitions were difficult to enforce, because golf was a game with no social distinctions. It was not just the common people who played; Mary, Queen of Scots was a golfer, and so was James VI, who is on record in the royal accounts-book as having lost a wager on the result of a match with one of his earls.

Golf was at first essentially a coastal game, played on the links — literally, the sandy turf which linked the countryside with the sea-shore.

Many Scottish courses, like the most famous of them all, the Old Course at St Andrews in Fife, are still laid out in these same basic conditions.

The Old Course has no trees, no flowering shrubs, no lakes, no ornamental landscaping. It is simply an uncompromising stretch of very well maintained coastal turf, with ridges and hidden hollows, a burn meandering across it, massive greens and fearsome sand-filled bunkers with names like Coffin, Grave and Hell.

While golf has spread from Scotland all over the world, St Andrews remains the game's spiritual but watchful home.

When one of the American astronauts played what amounted to a bunker shot on the gravelly surface of the moon, the Royal and Ancient Golf Club of St Andrews sent him a congratulatory message, but at the same time pointed out that an infraction of the rules had been noted from 240,000 miles away.

The courses at Gleneagles Hotel attract golfers from all over the world

in its basically 12th-century church, the elegant Nethergate and Marketgate, and restored houses with carved 'marriage lintels' over the doors, recording the initials and often the marriage dates of the couples who first lived in them.

🚗 *THE EAST NEUK towns are on the A917 east of Leven.*

FALKLAND
North-east Fife

The glory of this little town at the foot of the rounded Lomond Hills is Falkland Palace, created in the time of the Stuart kings and still a royal property today, although the splendidly restored buildings and furnished state rooms are open to the public through the National Trust for Scotland.

Generations of Stuart monarchs and their courtiers, from the time of James II in the 14th century onwards, loved to hunt in the forests around Falkland, and the palace was a favourite royal residence.

James V's French stonemasons added to it in Renaissance style; but after the court moved to London in 1603, the palace gradually fell into decay, before a grand rebuilding programme was put under way in the 1880s.

In terms of meticulous restoration, the rest of Falkland matches its palace. Town mansions, shops, cottages, workshops and taverns of the 17th to 19th centuries occupy the central area, which was Scotland's first-ever specially designated Conservation Area.

🚗 *FALKLAND is on the A912, 5 miles north of Glenrothes.*

This recreated schoolroom is part of the fascinating Angus Folk Museum housed in Kirkwynd Cottages, Glamis

GLAMIS
Angus

The grandest building in Angus is Glamis Castle, home of the Earls of Strathmore since 1372, and famous for its literary connection with Macbeth, courtesy of William Shakespeare's tragic play. It is built of delicately-shaded red sandstone, with a roofline which is a riot of slim, slate-roofed corbelled towers.

The heart of the castle, with its 15-ft thick walls, pre-dates by many centuries the main building completed in 1687. It has valuable collections of furniture, tapestries and china; outside, there are formal gardens and a nature trail in the wooded parkland, and a hugely ornamented sundial on one of the lawns.

In the village of Glamis, the National Trust for Scotland looks after the 17th-century Kirkwynd Cottages, home of the extensive Angus Folk Collection; the last of Scotland's handloom linen-weavers can also be seen at work.

🚗 *GLAMIS is off the A94, 25 miles north-east of Perth.*

THE HILLFOOTS
Clackmannan

Laid out along the very foot of the Ochil Hills, five villages and towns here are noted for their mild weather, colourful gardens and well-restored houses.

Blairlogie is a compact village sheltering below crags and gorse-banks. Once a year, visitors crowd its narrow lanes when more than a dozen village gardens are open to view.

Alva's fortunes were founded at the very end of the 18th century when the first of several woollen mills was built. In the 1820s, Alva Burn was

tapped to provide water-power for the mills, and a spectacular footpath follows the pipeline, high above a precipitous ravine, up into the Ochils.

In Menstrie, the 16th-century castle has been ingeniously converted into flats and a public library: but it also houses the Nova Scotia Room. This commemorates the founding, in the reign of James VI and I, of the colony of Nova Scotia — New Scotland — in Canada.

Coats of arms are displayed of the baronetcies of Nova Scotia created in the hope that their holders would finance the colony's development. Sir William Alexander of Menstrie was the prime mover of the scheme.

At Tillicoultry, the Mill Glen nature trail climbs steeply past waterfalls to open moorland. And at Dollar, paths and footbridges in a wooded glen lead up to the fine viewpoint of Castle Campbell, a part-restored 15th to 17th-century fortress of the Campbell Earls of Argyll.

🚗 *THE HILLFOOTS road is the A91, north-east of Stirling.*

LAKE OF MENTEITH
Stirling

Although there are smaller, artificially created lakes elsewhere, this is the only stretch of natural inland water in Scotland which is not called a loch.

At Port of Menteith, the square-towered parish church, the white buildings of a lakeside hotel and the water's-edge screen of trees with the wooded Menteith Hills in the background are all reflected in the still waters.

Port of Menteith is an angling resort, and in hard winters curling matches are sometimes held on the ice.

A ferry runs to Inchmahome, largest of the lake's wooded islands.

This is a remarkably peaceful place, where the ruins of a 13th-century Augustinian priory are maintained as an ancient monument among well-trimmed lawns.

Inchmahome is most famous as the hideout — during an English invasion in 1547 — of the infant Mary, Queen of Scots. She was brought here secretly for a few days before being moved, for greater safety, across the Channel to France.

🚗 *THE LAKE OF MENTEITH is off the A81, 6 miles east of Aberfoyle.*

LOCH KATRINE
Stirling

Visitors started coming in great numbers to admire the rugged Highland scenery here after Sir Walter Scott's ballad *The Lady of the Lake* — the lake being Loch Katrine — was published in 1810. He used the district again as the setting for his best-selling novel *Rob Roy*.

The most spectacular approach to Loch Katrine is over the Duke's Road from Aberfoyle, originally built in 1820 by the Duke of Montrose to provide a carriage-route for tourists. It winds over a pass through birchwoods and forest plantations, then plunges down past Loch Achray to the turn-off for Loch Katrine itself.

The loch and its entire hilly catchment area are owned by Strathclyde Regional Council's water department, which provides a visitor centre where the public road ends at Trossachs Pier.

Summer cruises to Stronachlachar at the far end of the loch are run by the elegant little turn-of-the-century steamer *Sir Walter Scott*. Walkers and cyclists can reach there by using the private road past Rob Roy MacGregor's birthplace at Glengyle.

🚗 *TROSSACHS PIER is on the A821, 7 miles north of Aberfoyle.*

LOCH LEVEN
Perth and Kinross

Extending to nearly 4000 acres, with seven islands of varying sizes, Loch Leven is a famous trout fishery and National Nature Reserve. Geese, ducks and swans winter in their thousands here.

The Lomond Hills sweep up to the east, and part of Benarty Hill to the south is occupied by the Vane Farm reserve of the Royal Society for the Protection of Birds. Gliders, using the air-currents over the hills, soar from Portmoak on the south-eastern side.

Kinross on the west side of the loch is the old county town. A lochside park is the starting point of ferry trips to the wooded Castle Island.

The basically 14th-century island fortress is famous as the prison where Mary, Queen of Scots was forced to abdicate in favour of her infant son James VI.

In 1568 she made a daring escape, only to meet imprisonment and death in England.

KINROSS is off the M9, 13 miles north of Dunfermline.

LOCH TAY
Perth and Kinross

Surrounded by mountains, this 15-mile loch is fed from the west by the united waters of the Lochay and the Dochart, which tumbles into the village of Killin in a series of famous rapids and rocky falls.

The main road along the north side runs below the looming 3984-ft bulk of Ben Lawers, where the National Trust for Scotland has a visitor centre and a notable reserve of arctic and alpine wildflowers.

Eventually, the road skirts the plantations of Drummond Hill Forest, with their network of high-level viewpoint walks, and arrives at the beautifully located and arranged village of Kenmore, built by the Earls and Marquesses of Breadalbane as an ornament at the entrance to Taymouth Castle.

The inn at Kenmore, built in 1572, is the oldest in Scotland; this is where the ceremonial opening of the Tay salmon season is celebrated every January.

A minor road turns back from the foot of the loch, along the southern shore past the old mill village of Acharn and the smaller angling resort of Ardeonaig, as it makes its way through woodlands and fields back towards Killin.

THE MAIN ROAD along Loch Tay is the A827 from Killin to Kenmore.

PERTH
Perth and Kinross

Spreading out from a mostly Georgian centre, Perth is built on both banks of the Tay, with riverside parks at the North and South Inch which have been public property since the 14th century.

The North Inch has a golf course and sports fields, behind which are the modern Bell's Sports Centre and the historic 16th-century Balhousie Castle which acts as the Black Watch museum.

The house called Branklyn at the foot of Kinnoull Hill has probably the finest town garden in the country, now maintained by the National Trust for Scotland.

Substantial villas are set in wooded grounds on the slopes of Kinnoull Hill. Another public park on the highest level above cliffs overlooking

Perth is spread over both banks of the River Tay and contains some interesting and historic buildings

the lower Tay provides outstanding views and is crossed by a multitude of footpaths.

Down in the town centre, St John's Kirk was the scene on 11 May 1559 of the most significant sermon ever preached in Scotland.

Unerringly catching the mood of the time, John Knox's fiery address from the pulpit set ablaze the forces of Reformation.

🚗 *PERTH is off the M90, 40 miles north of Edinburgh.*

PITLOCHRY
Perth and Kinross

This is a beautifully situated holiday resort in the mountain and forest-flanked valley of the River Tummel, which was dammed as part of a hydro-electric scheme to create the attractive and gently winding Loch Faskally.

A fish ladder allowing salmon to make their way to the traditional spawning grounds upstream is included in the visitor centre at Pitlochry dam.

There is a modern Festival Theatre on the far bank of the Tummel. Pitlochry is an angling and golfing centre. There are forest walks by Loch Faskally and the smaller Loch Dunmore, and up to the viewpoint summit of Craigower. And beauty spots like the wooded ravine at the battlefield of Killiecrankie are within easy reach.

🚗 *PITLOCHRY is off the A9, 26 miles north of Perth.*

ST ANDREWS
North-east Fife

As well as being the home of golf — with no fewer than four 18-hole courses owned by a public trust on the world-famous links behind the two-mile West Sands — St Andrews

97

St Andrews has Scotland's oldest university, founded in 1411

has Scotland's oldest university, which was founded in 1411 and still spreads all over the town in a series of handsome colleges and quadrangles.

The ruined cathedral, dedicated to Scotland's patron saint, gave the town its name; by the time it was completed in 1318, it was the largest church ever to be built in Scotland.

St Andrews Castle, with the grisly Bottle Dungeon from which there was positively no escape, was built in the 12th century. It became the fortress of Cardinal Beaton, who had several Reformers burned at the stake before being himself assassinated in the castle in 1546.

Fortunately, there are many happier places in St Andrews — a neatly proportioned town plan, carefully restored buildings, the finest city gate in Scotland at the West Port, pleasant walks on the wooded Lade Braes above the Kinness Burn, a botanic garden, holiday facilities and the modern Byre Theatre, on the same site as the original theatre, which really did begin its working life as the cow-shed of a dairy farm.

ST ANDREWS is on the A91, 10 miles east of Cupar.

SCONE PALACE
Perth and Kinross

The present mansion-house here, completed in 1808 for the Earl of Mansfield, stands on the site of a 16th-century predecessor whose main gateway is still in place. But the historic significance of Scone goes far further back in time.

In the grounds is the site of an ancient capital of the Picts, and Scone was the place where the kings of Scotland were crowned, from the 9th century until Charles II's coronation in 1651.

The palace is splendidly furnished, with collections of paintings, china, ivory, clocks and needlework on display. Its grounds feature formal gardens and a very extensive pinetum.

SCONE PALACE is on the A93, 2 miles north of Perth.

STIRLING
Stirling

Even today, this is a town in an important location, on the main road and rail routes north. But its position was much more significant in earlier centuries, when its fortress on a huge, unscaleable crag faced west over the all but trackless marshes round the meanders of the River Forth, and all land traffic to the Highlands was forced to pass this way.

The present Stirling Castle was built by the Stuart kings, and it is open to the public as one of Scotland's most impressive ancient monuments.

The castle is supported by many other substantial buildings in 'the top of the town', which is currently being revitalised; high-level walks around the hill offer outstanding views.

On Abbey Craig across the Forth there is a Victorian monument, in the form of a 220-ft tower with display rooms, to Sir William Wallace, victor at the Battle of Stirling Bridge in 1297 over an invading English army.

Dramatically floodlit, like the castle itself, at night, it has an eagle's-eye view over no fewer than seven battlefields.

Most famous of these, south of the town, is Bannockburn, where the National Trust for Scotland has a major exhibition on the site of Robert the Bruce's final and decisive victory over Edward II in 1314, thereby guaranteeing Scotland's independence once and for all.

STIRLING is off the M9, 26 miles north-east of Glasgow.

Stirling Castle from the approach across the gardens. The castle houses the museum of the Argyll and Sutherland Highlanders

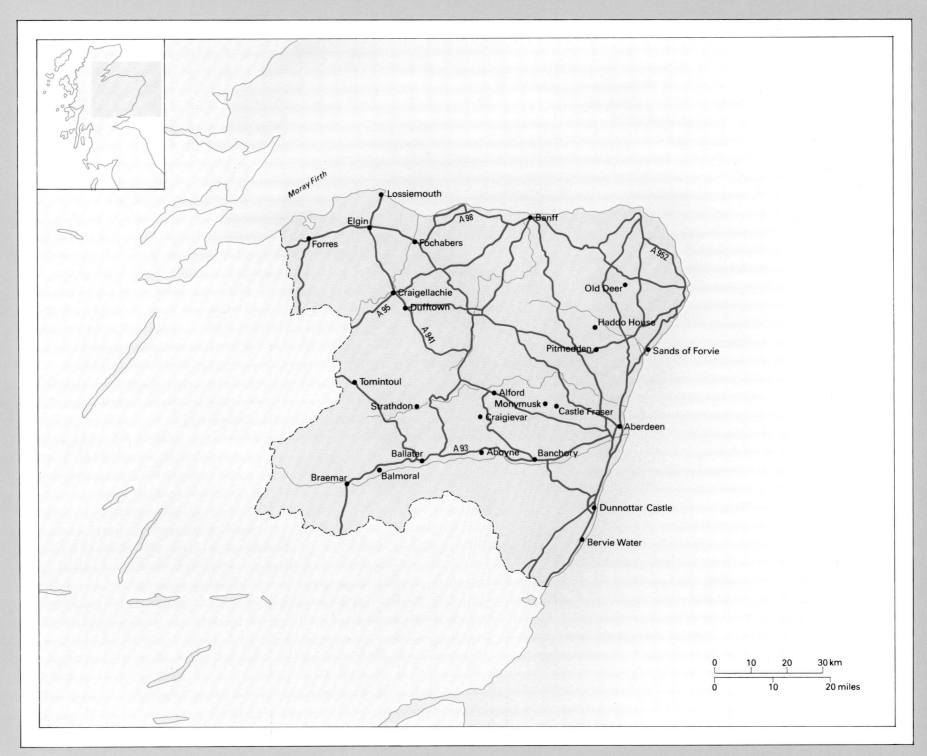

Moray Firth

Lossiemouth

Elgin
Forres
Fochabers
A 98
Banff
A 952

Craigellachie
Dufftown
A 95
A 941
Old Deer

Haddo House

Pitmedden
Sands of Forvie

Tomintoul

Alford
Monymusk
Castle Fraser

Strathdon
Craigievar

Aberdeen

Ballater
A 93
Aboyne
Banchory

Braemar
Balmoral

Dunnottar Castle

Bervie Water

0   10   20   30 km

0   10   20 miles

Grampian Region

Elgin's ruined 13th-century cathedral is its most famous building. It was burned out in the raid by the Earl of Buchan which was his reply to a sentence of excommunication

*T*HIS NORTH-EASTERN corner of Scotland takes its name from a range of mountains which, in their turn, are a misprinted version of the Latin name *Mons Graupius*, a famous battle between the Romans and the Picts whose actual site is still in debate.

The heart of Grampian is undoubtedly Royal Deeside, where tourists and wealthy mansion-house builders took their cue from Queen Victoria and Prince Albert, the creators of Balmoral as the Royal Family's Scottish home.

But there had been castle-builders here generations before: not only the barons who raised fortresses like Kildrummy and Corgarff, but also the prosperous merchants and landowners who commissioned local architects and masons to design some of Scotland's finest stately homes at places like Crathes, Castle Fraser and Craigievar.

There are rugged mountains inland, like Lochnagar with its towering cliffs; old-established pinewoods and newer plantations of spruce; lesser heathery summits crossed by winding hill roads like the Lecht, Cabrach and Cairn o'Mount, and many well-run, productive farms.

As a contrast, Grampian also includes the bustling city of Aberdeen and a well-settled coast where holiday resorts and fishing ports at Stonehaven, Peterhead, Fraserburgh, Banff and Macduff share the extensive sands, cliffs and headlands with active or retired fishing villages like Pennan and Gardenstown, Findochty, Burghead and Findhorn.

ABERDEEN
City of Aberdeen

Visitors to Aberdeen airport, where helicopters run all-day shuttle services to production platforms far out in the North Sea, may have the impression that this is little more than a modern oil city.

But the place the Vikings called *Apardion* has civic history going back to the early 12th century. Its extensive public parks can be traced to a charter signed in 1319 by Robert the Bruce, outlining the Freedom Lands of Aberdeen. And the fortunes made from the Baltic trade financed many of the city's fine public and private buildings.

Despite its not entirely undeserved reputation for north-east hard-headedness, Aberdeen is lavish in many unexpected ways. It may be the Granite City, for instance, but in summer it is also the City of Roses — on the first Rose Day in 1983, a quarter of a million rosebuds were handed out free.

Parks, gardens, golf courses and a two-mile beach make sure that Aberdeen has plenty of fresh air and elbow-room; but the historic centre is well worth exploring too.

St Nicholas Church in Union Street has a carillon of 48 bells, the largest in Britain. Wealthy merchants like Provost Ross and Provost Skene built themselves grand town houses which are now museums: Provost Ross's house in the Shiprow includes displays on Aberdeen's fishing and harbour trades, and on the National Trust for Scotland's properties all over Grampian.

Most of Aberdeen's university buildings are in Old Aberdeen, a copybook example of Georgian restoration. Notable earlier buildings there include St Machar's Cathedral and the original King's College of 1505.

Older still is the splendid Gothic-arched Brig o'Balgownie over the River Don, opened in 1329 and now one of Scotland's finest medieval structures still in everyday use.

ABERDEEN is 117 miles north of Edinburgh.

ABOYNE
Kincardine and Deeside

After being established in the 1670s, the village here became the focal point of the River Dee timber trade. Pinewood logs cut in the Forest of Glentanar were assembled at Aboyne into rafts which were floated down-river to Aberdeen.

Retaining its granite houses overlooking the green where Aboyne

Aberdeen was a thriving port by the 13th century. Today it is the largest oil field supply base in Scotland

Neo-classical Aberdeen: Union Street, built in the 1800s

Highland Games are held every year, the village was rebuilt and extended in mid-Victorian times by Sir William Cunliffe Brookes, a millionaire banker who became the proprietor of Glentanar estate, one of many incoming Royal Deeside lairds.

In and around Aboyne, there are facilities for golf and angling, water-skiing on Aboyne Loch and gliding on Dinnet Moor.

An informative visitor centre is provided at Braeloine in Glentanar, at the start of a network of very attractive riverside, farm and woodland walks.

🚗 *ABOYNE is 31 miles west of Aberdeen on the A93.*

ALFORD
Gordon

This market town is in the Howe of Alford, a low-lying area around the windings of the River Don where farms and wooded estates give way to forest plantations and rounded open hills.

The Grampian Transport Museum

is located here; undoubted star of its display is the Craigievar Express, a steam-powered tricycle built by a remarkable local postman, Andrew Lawson, and put on the roads in 1897.

Nearby, the redundant main line Alford station has been restored as a local railway museum. From it, a narrow-gauge railway runs regular leisurely services into the two country parks — Haughton House and Murray Park — which bound Alford to the north. Murray Park was presented to the people of Alford in 1935 by a highly-regarded north-east poet, Charles Murray.

In both parks there are nature trails through birch, conifer and mixed woodland where roe deer browse.

Provost Skene's 16th-century house on Flourmill Lane contains a folk museum

🚗 *ALFORD is 26 miles west of Aberdeen on the A944.*

BALLATER
Kincardine and Deeside

A town built of granite to a regular, rectangular plan, Ballater is on a fan of level ground in a bend of the River Dee. There are wooded hills all around — notably just behind the town at Craigendarroch, where footpaths climbing through birch, oak and pinewood lead to a summit viewpoint which opens up a splendid Deeside panorama.

As the idea of Royal Deeside gathered momentum, so the 18th-century settlement of Ballater grew in size and significance as a holiday resort.

The riverside land south-west of the town is laid out as an attractive golf course. There is angling on the rivers and on various nearby lochs.

A four-mile walk heads east along the track-bed of the old Deeside Railway to Cambus o'May. Another walk by the wooded riverside follows what was intended to be an extension of the railway westwards to Braemar; but Queen Victoria vetoed it, because the line would have brought the trains directly in sight of Balmoral.

🚗 *BALLATER is 42 miles west of Aberdeen on the A93.*

BALMORAL
Kincardine and Deeside

It was in 1847 that Queen Victoria and Prince Albert, having a fairly miserable late-summer holiday on an Inverness-shire estate where the rain battered down all day and the cloud-capped mountains were already sprinkled with snow, heard that the weather on Deeside was bright, sunny and dry.

For the next few years, they rented

Balmoral, on a bend in the River Dee between Ballater and Braemar; and in 1852 Prince Albert finally bought the whole Balmoral estate.

In 1853 building work started on the present granite castle with its 100-ft turreted tower. The Prince collaborated with Aberdeen architect William Smith on the detail design; and with the creation of new gardens as well as new houses for the staff, Balmoral was on its way to becoming what it still is today — a model but working estate of hill, forest and farmland.

It remains the Royal Family's private Scottish home; but the beautifully wooded grounds and gardens are open to visitors during most of May, June and July, and there is an exhibition in the ballroom.

Balmoral Estates have also cooperated with the Scottish Wildlife Trust in providing public access to a spectacular 6350-acre mountain reserve which includes the major summits of Lochnagar. The reserve's visitor centre is near Loch Muick, at the end of a minor road south-west of Ballater.

🚗 *BALMORAL is 48 miles west of Aberdeen off the A93.*

BANCHORY
Kincardine and Deeside

Golf, sea-trout and salmon fishing are among the attractions of this inland Deeside holiday resort, and Banchory is also an excellent centre for walking. There are wandering paths all around it, in natural woodlands and in Forestry Commission plantations of pine, spruce and larch.

An unexpected product of the district is lavender, and there are guided tours of the Ingasetter factory which distills it into perfumes.

About three miles down the valley of the Dee, Crathes Castle is one of

the grandest properties of the National Trust for Scotland. Although the castle itself was built towards the end of the 16th century, the Burnett lairds — originally de Burnards — who owned it until 1952 were granted the lands here by Robert the Bruce.

He appointed his supporter Alexander de Burnard a royal forester; and the hunting horn which, according to tradition, was presented as the badge of office still hangs in the High Hall of Crathes today.

There are nature trails in the well-wooded 595-acre Crathes grounds. But Crathes is more famous for its eight inter-linked gardens with their varying colour and landscape themes. Lawns and topiary-worked yew hedges planted in Queen Anne's time add to the attractions of one of northeast Scotland's finest open-to-the-public estates.

🚗 *BANCHORY is 18 miles south west of Aberdeen on the A93.*

BANFF
Banff and Buchan

A lively Preservation Society makes sure that the architectural heritage of this old county town is maintained. Houses, churches, inns and public buildings are mostly of the 17th and 18th centuries.

Duff House, outside the town, is a Georgian extravaganza designed by William Adam for the 1st Earl of Fife; but an icy row between them, over a structural fault, meant that the building was never completed according to its original plans.

The mansion-house is open to the public as an ancient monument; its grounds include a golf course by the River Deveron and a woodland walk

Balmoral Castle, bought and rebuilt by Prince Albert in the 1850s

The L-shaped tower house of Crathes Castle contains some outstanding examples of painted ceilings

up-river to the ravine crossed by the high-arched Bridge of Alvah.

Over the bridge, an old livestock-drovers' track leads through Mont-coffer Wood back to Macduff, the rival town built opposite Banff on the far side of the river-mouth.

Unlike Banff's own harbour, Macduff's remains a busy and prosperous fishing port. Sea angling and water-skiing are also catered for at Macduff. There is a fine viewpoint in front of the high-set parish church, and a striking war memorial tower rises on another hilltop.

At Tarlair, an open-air swimming pool with attached boating lake is overlooked by an adventurously laid-out clifftop golf course.

BANFF is 47 miles north west of Aberdeen.

BERVIE WATER
Kincardine and Deeside

This unobtrusive river is formed from a number of streams draining the hillsides of Drumtochty Forest, and gathers more tiny tributaries as it flows through the farmlands of the Mearns in a series of sweeping curves which are themselves made up of in-numerable smaller bends.

Robert Burns's father was a farmer's son hereabouts before moving to Edinburgh and latterly as a market gardener to Alloway. Several of Burns's relations are buried in the leafy churchyard at Glenbervie.

Downstream at Arbuthnott, one of Scotland's most notable rural chur-ches — St Ternan's, based on a restored 13th-century chancel — stands above one of the Bervie Water's beautiful wooded curves.

In the churchyard there is a memorial to James Leslie Mitchell — otherwise the novelist Lewis Grassic Gibbon — whose *Sunset Song* trilogy, familiar from television, recalled the hard life earlier this cen-tury in the hill-farm country to the north.

The river reaches the sea at In-verbervie, birthplace of the great clipper-ship designer Hercules Linton. In 1872 his *Cutty Sark* won the most famous of all the races to bring back the first high-value shipload of the new season's China tea.

Sir Francis Chichester came to Inverbervie in 1969 to unveil the striking Linton memorial.

INVERBERVIE is on the A92, 10 miles south of Stonehaven.

BRAEMAR
Kincardine and Deeside

The highest village on Royal Deeside, Braemar is a place whose story tradi-tionally goes back to the 10th cen-tury, when Kenneth II is said to have brought his courtiers here on a deer-hunt, leaving the wooded hill which rises east of the village — Creag Choinnich, or Kenneth's Crag — named after him.

A much later hunting party was the occasion when the Earl of Mar raised the Jacobite standard to announce the start of the 1715 Rising.

Queen Victoria and Prince Albert came to the Braemar Gathering dur-ing their first holiday at Balmoral in 1848, and established it as the pre-eminent sporting and social event of the Deeside season — which, with the Royal Family always in attendance, it remains to the present day.

Rather more quietly, Robert Louis Stevenson brought his family here in the summer of 1881, renting a holiday cottage on the Glenshee road. He spent most of the days writing, and by the evening fireside would read aloud the latest completed chapters of *Treasure Island*.

In the valley, the historic 17th-century Braemar Castle is open to visitors during the summer. Higher up, there are magnificent views towards the Cairngorms from the bir-chwood and juniper reserve on the hillside of Morrone.

BRAEMAR is 16 miles west of Ballater on the A93.

Malt Whisky

Connoisseurs of whisky give classic status to the unblended 'single malts', whose brand names are also the geographical locations of the distilleries which produce them.

What gives each single malt whisky its characteristic and never-duplicated taste is not just the standard processes of barley-malting followed by mashing followed by fermenting, distilling and maturing. The pure water of Highland burns tumbling down peaty hillsides is simply not available anywhere else in the world — and every individual distillery has its own carefully guarded supply.

Six distilleries in Grampian have combined to offer visitor facilities and guided tours on the Malt Whisky Trail, where history, tradition, explanation of processes and a complimentary 'dram' are all part of the attraction.

Glenfiddich attracts over 90,000 visitors in a typical year; The Glenlivet — in a district which was originally a hotbed of illegal distilling — was granted that significant definite article in 1880; at Glenfarclas the Grants are the only malt whisky dynasty to have passed ownership on in an unbroken line from father to son, since the June day in 1870 when John Grant, while more concerned at that time with clipping sheep, noted almost as an afterthought in his diary that the first 320 gallons had been produced in his lately-acquired

The Glenfiddich Distillery pagodas — the name given to the pyramid-like roofs over the malt-drying kiln

A whisky connoisseur's paradise: the cellars at Glenfiddich Distillery

distillery.

At Tamdhu the visitor centre is in the station built for the distillery on a now-abandoned railway; Glen Grant is in the whisky town of Rothes, beside the angling waters of the Spey; and Strathisla at Keith has claims to being the oldest working distillery north of the Highland Line.

Old or new, and whether or not they actually continue to malt their own barley over peat fires, most distilleries retain that famous architectural feature which identifies them from miles away: the special roof over the malt-drying kiln which is always described as a pagoda.

CASTLE FRASER
Gordon

In 16th and 17th-century Aberdeenshire there were two families of architects and master masons — the Bells and the Leipers — who were both involved in the creation of the spectacular Castle Fraser, on the edge of the middle valley of the Don.

This is the largest of the National Trust for Scotland's Castles of Mar, a building extended from a smaller original in 1575, for a Fraser laird after whom the square Michael Tower is named.

Later additions up to 1636 gave the castle an ornamented roofline of remarkable elegance — delicate dormer windows, cornices, crow-stepped gables, corbelled turrets and a massive heraldic carving with a modest addition of the date 1617 plus 'I. Bel' — John Bell, the self-effacing master designer.

Inside the castle, there are appropriate furnishings, portraits and needlework to be admired; and the Round Tower is topped by a balustraded viewing platform looking out over the wooded parkland grounds.

CASTLE FRASER is 3 miles south of Kemnay.

CRAIGELLACHIE
Moray

Well-known to anglers for its salmon-beats on the River Spey, this is a whisky distillers' and coopers' village of Victorian granite, taking its name from the wooded cliff across the Spey which marked the traditional eastern boundary of the Clan Grant lands.

Across this stretch of water, the master bridge builder Thomas Telford built one of the most graceful bridges in Scotland.

With a 150-ft cast-iron span and four 'chess-piece' towers, his Craigellachie bridge was completed in 1815 and remains open to pedestrians — a fine industrial monument as well as an ornament to the landscape.

CRAIGELLACHIE is 13 miles south of Elgin on the A941.

CRAIGIEVAR
Gordon

Looking over its hillside parkland, midway between the valleys of the Dee and the Don, Craigievar is perhaps the most perfect 17th-century Scottish castle, in the ornamentation of its upper storeys and the uncluttered purity of its basic tower-like design.

There are no subsidiary wings or other buildings to divert the eye as it gazes up at the turreted skyline and balustraded rooftop platform.

Craigievar was almost certainly another masterpiece to the design of John Bell. It was completed in 1626 for William Forbes, one of Aberdeen's richest Baltic merchants, and remained a family home until it was bought by the National Trust for Scotland in 1963.

All the major rooms are open to visitors. Many have intricate moulded-plaster ceilings, and plaster is also used for the imposing Royal Arms over the fireplace in the medieval-style hall.

CRAIGIEVAR is off the A980, 6 miles south of Alford.

DUFFTOWN
Moray

In 1817 James Duff, 4th Earl of Fife, established a town on the hillside above the meeting of the Dullan Water and the River Fiddich.

Dufftown was therefore ideally situated in time and place to take advantage of the change in whisky

The outstanding ceiling in the Great Hall at Craigievar Castle

distilling from a largely illegal adventure to a substantial taxpaying industry which occurred a few years later; south-west of the town, the Dullan Water runs through Glen Rinnes, whose rounded hills had sheltered many an illicit whisky still.

Dufftown is now the heart of the malt whisky country, and Glenfiddich distillery's visitor centre is the busiest in Scotland.

But Dufftown's history goes back much further. The first church in the Kirktown of Mortlach is said to have been founded in the 6th century, and the present, much-restored church has old Pictish symbol stones on display.

From Mortlach, a footpath up the wooded Dullan valley makes for a delicate waterfall known as the Linen Apron, and the sturdy rock formation of the Giant's Chair.

North of the town, the basically 13th-century Balvenie Castle is open as an ancient monument; and the history of the area is summed up in a museum in the baronial clock tower in the square.

🚗 *DUFFTOWN is 18 miles south east of Elgin on the A941.*

DUNNOTTAR CASTLE
Kincardine and Deeside

Occupying the summit plateau of a prodigious cliff-bound rock, Dunnottar is an all but island fortress on the coast south of the holiday resort of Stonehaven.

A stronghold to be coveted by either side, it was attacked and defended heartily during all the English wars. The present castle was started in the 14th century by Sir William Keith, Earl Marischal of Scotland.

With defences which had been continually strengthened over the years, Dunnottar was the last place to hold out against Cromwell's army, surrendering with honours, after an eight-month siege, in May 1652.

The besiegers had expected to find, in the castle, the Regalia of Scotland — the crown, sceptre and sword of state; but in a magnificently daring escapade, they had already been smuggled out, and were safely hidden in the parish church of Kinneff, a few miles down the coast.

Kinneff's historic church is well restored, and has an exhibition on its most exciting episode.

Dunnottar itself was partly dismantled after the Jacobite Rising of 1715; but much of it was restored in an extensive private project started in 1925. It is open to visitors, still a place with massive defences, in a stunning location with wide-ranging North Sea views.

🚗 *DUNNOTTAR is 2 miles south of Stonehaven.*

ELGIN
Moray

This is the market town for the farms and estates in the Moray lowlands, with the River Lossie meandering along its original northern boundary.

Much of Elgin, like the Greek-pillared church in a widening of the High Street, was built in Georgian style. But the most famous building here is the ruined 13th-century cathedral.

In 1390 it was burned out in a raid by the Earl of Buchan, known with good reason as the 'Wolf of Badenoch'. This was his typical riposte to a well-deserved sentence of excommunication.

The cathedral was rebuilt; but it was brusquely treated after the Reformation. Now preserved as an ancient monument, it remains strikingly handsome even in decay.

Elgin Museum has a notable geological collection as well as displays on local regiments; and a meal-mill restored to working condition is open to visitors during the summer.

🚗 *ELGIN is 67 miles north west of Aberdeen.*

FOCHABERS
Moray

The conservation area at the heart of this 'planned' town on the east bank of the Spey is mostly Georgian, although there is also an impressive Victorian school.

Fochabers folk museum is noted for its collection of horse-drawn carriages. Across the Spey bridge to the west, Baxters of Speyside is a food-processing firm with a world-wide export trade, whose visitor centre includes the rebuilt Victorian shop from the High Street of Fochabers where the business started on a much more modest scale.

The Winding Walks in Speymouth Forest wander through a glen with rhododendrons, birches and mixed conifer plantations. A high-level viewpoint known as The Peeps looks down along the High Street, and over the wooded farmlands of lower Speyside.

🚗 *FOCHABERS is 9 miles south east of Elgin on the A96.*

FORRES
Moray

In Shakespeare's *Macbeth*, the second scene is in 'a camp near Forres', following on the famous opening when the witches chant through the thunder and lightning of an

The seemingly impregnable position of Dunnottar Castle forced Cromwell's army to besiege it

anonymous 'open place'. Traditionally, this is identified as the Hardmuir west of the town.

But Forres, built on both sides of the little Mosset Burn, has much more to offer than the brief encounter with great drama. It is a town of parks and gardens, where the wooded summits of the small-scale Cluny Hills have

footpaths towards a viewpoint tower set up to commemorate Nelson's victory at Trafalgar.

One of Scotland's finest early sculptured monuments stands beside the Kinloss road. Sueno's Stone is a 20-ft pillar with detailed carvings of warriors in battle array.

Four miles west of Forres, the

Brodies of Brodie — now in their 25th generation of chiefs — have been landowners since 1160. Their 16th-century Brodie Castle, with its collections of furniture, paintings and porcelain, is now the property of the National Trust for Scotland. There is a woodland walk in the grounds, skirting a four-acre ornamental lake.

South of Brodie Castle are the extensive forests and farmlands of the Earl of Moray's Darnaway estate. Guided tours are arranged in summer from the visitor centre at Tearie Farm, and include the basically 15th-century Darnaway Castle.

FORRES is 11 miles west of Elgin on the A96.

110 **The Blue Drawing-room at Brodie Castle, showing the fine barrel-vaulted plasterwork ceiling**

HADDO HOUSE
Gordon

Although Haddo House is still the centre of a privately-run estate, the mansion and its gardens are now owned by the National Trust for Scotland, and 180 acres of the wooded grounds make up a local-authority country park.

William Adam designed Haddo House in the 1730s for the 2nd Earl of Aberdeen. Its restrained Georgian style was altered in detail during a remodelling in the 1880s, when the Gothic chapel with its Burne-Jones stained-glass windows was added.

The main rooms, still furnished in distinguished style, are open to visitors. Haddo House Choral and Operatic Society, founded in 1945, continues to produce operas, concerts and plays in the late-Victorian maplewood hall.

The country park consists of lawns and grazing land, picnic areas in a sheltered rhododendron wood, enough broadleaved and conifer species to justify the Tree Trail, and other footpaths round an ornamental lake which is also a popular roost for wildfowl.

HADDO HOUSE is 6 miles north east of Oldmeldrum.

LOSSIEMOUTH
Moray

Until a few hundred years ago, there was not only no town at Lossiemouth — the mouth of the River Lossie was also some distance away. The sea-coast ran much closer to the county town of Elgin, which had its salt-water port at a place called Spynie.

But a massive sand and shingle bar built up, cutting Spynie off from the sea and creating a vast inland lagoon. In 1698 the town council of Elgin had to buy land for a new harbour at what is now Lossiemouth, and the town built up steadily around it.

The lagoon and its marshland fringe were drained for farmland in the 1880s, and the Spynie Canal built for the project still flows through Lossiemouth today.

An excellent museum near the harbour has comprehensive displays on Lossiemouth and its fishing industry through the years.

It also includes the re-created study of Lossiemouth's most famous son — Ramsay MacDonald, Britain's first Labour prime minister. A hillside memorial to him is a fine viewpoint over the old Seatown, the remains of the lagoon, the sand-dunes and beaches — reached by a long foot-bridge — on its seaward side, and the plantations of Lossie Forest stretching to the south-east.

West of the town there are more beaches, a picnic area and a fine golf course, which all have a grandstand view of the RAF planes on training flights from Lossiemouth aerodrome.

LOSSIEMOUTH is 5 miles north of Elgin.

MONYMUSK
Gordon

A little way back from the south bank of the Don, where the river finally shakes itself free of the hills and comes into lowland country, Monymusk is centred on a square of very attractively restored cottages around the village green. They were remodelled at the turn of the century by Sir Arthur Grant of Monymusk estate.

Towering above the cottages, however, is the real architectural glory of the village — the 12th-century Norman church of sandstone and granite, carefully restored in the 1930s and also given some good modern stained glass.

In the porch is a reminder that there was a religious house on this site long before the present one. The Monymusk Stone dates from the time of the Culdee priests of the earlier Celtic church which faded before the advance of the disciplines of Rome.

MONYMUSK is on the B993, 10 miles east of Alford.

OLD DEER
Banff and Buchan

Until the Reformation, this little grey-stone village at a double bend of the South Ugie Water was best known for the 13th-century abbey nearby. The buildings then fell into decay, and were almost completely destroyed by a Victorian landowner who ransacked them to build a family burial aisle.

The ruins have now been reinstated as an ancient monument, standing peacefully among riverside lawns.

Immediately east of Old Deer, Aden House was once the centre of an extensive farming estate. But the Russell lairds of Aden fell on hard

Haddo House, home of the Earls of Aberdeen, where concerts are regularly performed

times, and the last of them sold out in 1937.

In the 1970s, 220 acres around the now-ruined mansion were transformed into Aden Country Park, one of the showpieces of Buchan. The totally restored home-farm buildings include one of the finest estate-history displays in Scotland.

🚗 *OLD DEER is 2 miles west of Mintlaw.*

PITMEDDEN
Gordon

Although most of the National Trust for Scotland's properties in Grampian feature the castles and mansion-houses, at Pitmedden the principal attraction is the re-created 17th-century Great Garden, first laid out for Sir Alexander Seton.

Its centrepiece is the series of parterres with low boxwood hedges

outlining patterns which are filled in with 40,000 flowers planted out every season. One of the designs shows Sir Alexander Seton's coat of arms; the others are based on drawings of the old gardens of Holyrood Palace in Edinburgh.

Elsewhere on the estate, restored farm buildings house a Museum of Farming Life. There are indoor displays of vintage farm equipment and outdoor collections of rare Scottish livestock breeds like the Rum pony, Soay and Boreray sheep from the far-out Atlantic rockstacks of St Kilda.

🚗 *PITMEDDEN is 5 miles east of Oldmeldrum.*

SANDS OF FORVIE
Gordon

Although there was a time when as many as 250 fishermen operated from

Collieston, this colourful little village of cottages scattered round a tidal bay is now mostly a holiday resort.

To the south, the cliffs with their one-time smugglers' caves gradually give way to a shoreline of extensive sand-dunes. From here to the estuary of the River Ythan is the Sands of Forvie nature reserve. Terns and eiders in huge numbers come here to nest, and wild geese winter in their thousands.

From Collieston, a footpath leads through the lonely heathland in the centre of the reserve, passing the ruined church of the lost village of Forvie, which now lies under the sands.

🚗 *COLLIESTON is on the B9003, 22 miles north east of Aberdeen.*

STRATHDON
Gordon

At Cock Bridge, where the Lecht road from Tomintoul plummets out of the

wild hill country above, the River Don is overlooked by the recently restored 16th-century Corgarff Castle, manned by troops till as late as the 1830s, in the government's efforts to stamp out the last traces of illicit whisky distilling.

Several miles down the winding and beautifully wooded course of the Don, Kildrummy Castle, like Corgarff, is an ancient monument, considered to be the finest of all the medieval fortresses in the north of Scotland, but partly dismantled after the Jacobite Rising of 1715.

The modern Kildrummy Castle, now a hotel, was built at the turn of the century. Between the two castles, the 'back den' is a series of water, shrub and alpine gardens.

Midway between Kildrummy and Corgarff, the village of Strathdon is where, every August, the Lonach Highlanders with shouldered pikes and in full Highland dress march round the mansion-houses of the district before the start of the Lonach Games in the riverside sports field.

🚗 *STRATHDON village is on the B973, 19 miles west of Alford.*

TOMINTOUL
Gordon

After a steep and winding climb from Cock Bridge, past the skiing grounds around its summit, the Lecht road continues to the highest village in the Highlands at Tomintoul.

This is a bright and airy, neatly laid-out place around a central square, still following the street-plan drawn up in 1776.

There is a local museum; a country walk explores the steeply wooded glen of the River Avon; and athletes congregate at Tomintoul in July for Scotland's highest Highland Games.

🚗 *TOMINTOUL is on the A939, 26 miles north-west of Ballater.*

The 17th-century gardens at Pitmedden were neglected until restored by the National Trust for Scotland

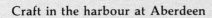
Craft in the harbour at Aberdeen

Index

INDEX

Acknowledgements

AA Picture Library: endpapers, 11, 18, 36, 37(b), 38(t,b), 39, 40, 50, 63, 64(t,b), 65, 68, 70(r), 76(t,b), 79, 80, 89, 91, 92, 96/7
Mary Evans Picture Library: 52(tl)
Courtesy Gleneagles Hotels: 93
Bill Howes Angling Photo Service: 10(t,b)
Anthony Lambert: 81
Cameron McNeish: title page, 4, 5, 7, 20/1, 22(t,b), 106(t,b)
Colin Molyneux: 103(t,b)
National Trust for Scotland: title verso 6, 8/9, 14, 19, 94, 105, 107
Scottish Tourist Board: contents, 3, 12, 13(l,r), 15, 17, 21, 23, 24, 25, 26, 27, 28/9, 31, 32, 33, 34, 37(t), 41, 42/3, 43, 45, 46, 47, 48, 48/9, 51, 52(tr,b), 53, 54/5, 57, 59, 60, 61, 62, 66, 67, 69, 70(l), 71, 73, 74, 75, 77, 78, 82/3, 84, 85, 87, 88, 90, 98, 99, 101, 104, 108/9, 110, 111, 112